Praise for Meghan Daum's

LIFE WOULD BE PERFECT
IF I LIVED IN THAT HOUSE

"Honest and endearing . . . richly drawn. . . . Daum captures the now-gone moment when real estate became a national obsession, chronicling the shared madness of those who could only take breaks from watching HGTV to discuss closing costs. . . . As she moves from coast to coast and in between, Daum is consistently relatable."
                                   —*Los Angeles Times Book Review*

"Daum has a rare gift in her ability to keep readers laughing through her own tears. . . . Her spirit is generous, her writing is buoyant, and her heart is open to all the ways in which a house holds the key to happiness. Perfection has nothing to do with it."   —*The New York Times Book Review*

"Suffused with humor and desire. . . . Alternately whimsical, philosophical and psychologically probing. . . . [An] enchanting, compelling memoir on the impossibility of resisting an irresistible object of desire."   —*The Miami Herald*

"Daum tackles real estate—or, more pointedly, the fixation, anxiety and magical thinking that often accompany it—with wit and a gift for self-parody. . . . Her prose has smarts, style and personality, but never turns pretentious. . . . It's a pleasure to read this author as she revisits comic misadventures and wrangles with a hot-button topic."   —*Time Out New York*

"Vividly described. . . . Daum exposes the modern real-estate-mad female underground, where open houses (visited in rabid two-women teams) are a seasonal blood sport, Zillow is a verb, and where remodeling a collapsing farmhouse into a writer's retreat could instantly, we imagine, transform us into the George Plimpton of the prairie."
—*The Atlantic Monthly*

"Entertaining. . . . Like a romantic comedy in which Daum always seems to rent Mr. Wrong. . . . Don't be surprised if you race through *Life Would Be Perfect* in a single night."
—*Richmond Times-Dispatch*

"Daum is the essential Generation X-er. . . . She radiates the eternal youthfulness and the fear of commitment that define her cohort. . . . *Life Would Be Perfect* is the memoir of how the wandering Ms. Daum finally put down some roots. . . . A great book." —*The Philadelphia Inquirer*

"Timely. . . . Daum [is] a fine writer—candid, reflective, stylish, fun and a bit prickly. Throughout the book, she offers an unflinching portrayal of her anxieties and her aspirations. . . . When she finally realizes that a house is not what will make her whole, you can't help but breathe a sigh of relief."
—Associated Press

"In this funny, horrifying (she came this close to buying a place near a roaring interstate because she was smitten with a landing) achingly honest memoir, Daum explores the way we wrap our identities in our surroundings, at one point wondering, 'Did the house look sexy on me?' Home truths, indeed." —*More*

Meghan Daum

LIFE WOULD BE PERFECT
IF I LIVED IN THAT HOUSE

Meghan Daum is the author of the essay collection *My Misspent Youth* and the novel *The Quality of Life Report*, a *New York Times* Notable Book. Her column on political, cultural, and social affairs appears weekly in the *Los Angeles Times* and is distributed nationally through the McClatchy news service. She has contributed to public radio's *Morning Edition, Marketplace,* and *This American Life,* and has written for numerous publications, including *The New Yorker, Harper's Magazine, GQ, Vogue, Harper's Bazaar,* and *The New York Times Book Review*. She lives in Los Angeles.

www.meghandaum.com

ALSO BY MEGHAN DAUM

The Quality of Life Report

My Misspent Youth

LIFE WOULD BE PERFECT
IF I LIVED IN THAT HOUSE

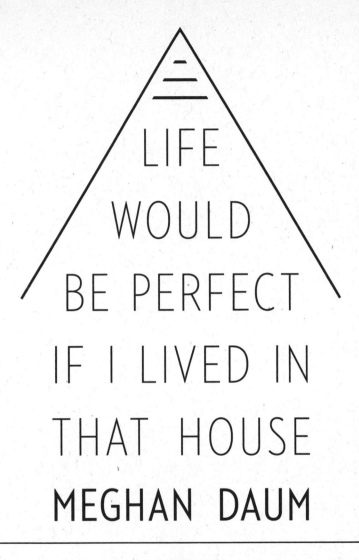

LIFE WOULD BE PERFECT IF I LIVED IN THAT HOUSE

MEGHAN DAUM

VINTAGE BOOKS
A DIVISION OF RANDOM HOUSE, INC.
NEW YORK

FIRST VINTAGE BOOKS EDITION, JUNE 2011

The Library of Congress has cataloged the Knopf edition as follows:
Daum, Meghan.
Life would be perfect if I lived in that house / Meghan Daum.—1st ed.
p. cm.
1. Daum, Meghan, 1970—Homes and haunts. 2. Real estate business—Humor. I. Title.
PS3604.A93Z46 2010
814'.6—dc22
2009037002

Vintage ISBN: 978-0-307-45484-3

Book design by Wesley Gott

www.vintagebooks.com

Printed in the United States of America
10 9 8 7 6 5 4 3 2 1

For my mother

LIFE WOULD BE PERFECT
IF I LIVED IN THAT HOUSE

PROLOGUE

Yesterday, a piece of my house came off in my hands. I don't mean that metaphorically. I banged the garbage can against an outside wall, and a piece of stucco about the size of a sheet of paper came ever so slightly loose. When I touched it, it fell gently into my palm. It was as if the house were giving me a lock of its hair, or perhaps coughing up phlegm. I was concerned, but it also happened that I was really busy that day. I just couldn't get into it with the stucco, not right then anyway. Also, I was coming up on my five-year anniversary of owning the house, and if there's anything I've learned in five years, it's this: if a piece of your house falls off and you don't know what to do with it, throwing it in the trash and forgetting about it is a perfectly viable option. And it so happened that the trash can was right there. Once upon a time I would have made a beeline to the yellow pages to look up "stucco replacement," but I've come a long way since then.

So has the house. I bought it in 2004, and as I write this, it's supposedly worth $100,000 less than what I paid for it. By the time you read this, it will probably be worth even less than that. I try not to care because if I cared too much, or even thought about it too much, I'd go insane. I've spent enough time here being insane, believe me. I was insane when I bought the place, and I went even more insane afterward. Then again, the whole world was high a few years ago. The whole world, or at least the whole country, was buying real estate and melting it down to liquid form and then injecting it into veins. For my part, it's tempting to say I succumbed to peer pressure, but it was really much more complicated than that. There is no object of desire quite like a house. Few things in this world are capable of eliciting such urgent, even painful, yearning. Few sentiments are at once as honest and as absurd as the one that moves us to declare: "Life would be perfect if I lived in that house."

I'm writing this book in homage to that sentiment, which is to say I'm telling the story of a very imperfect life lived among very imperfect houses.

A large part of that story, of course, involves the house that is now falling apart in my hands, the gist of which is basically this: In 2004, I was among the nearly six million Americans who purchased real estate. Like roughly a quarter of them, I was a single woman (single men don't buy houses nearly as often), and I was making the leap for the first time. Again, this was a time when the real estate market had reached a frenzy that surpassed even the tech boom of the mid-1990s. It was scarcely possible back then to attend a party or even get your teeth cleaned without falling into a conversation about real estate: its significance, its desirability, its increasing aura of unattainability. My dental hygienist, for example, had robust opinions about reverse mortgages.

Like many of my friends and neighbors, I attended so many open houses and made such a complete study of the Multiple Listing Service that the homes on the market seemed like human beings. We discussed the quirks and prices of these properties as though we were gossiping about our neighbors. At the risk of making a perverse and offensive comparison, I truly don't think I'd observed so much absorption with one topic since the attacks of September 11, 2001. As in those chilling days, we could literally speak of nothing else. People who had never put a thought toward home ownership were being seduced by record-low interest rates and "creative" financing plans. People who'd happily owned their homes for years were doubling and tripling their equity and suddenly realizing they could cash out or trade up. If the jolt of the fall of 2001 had rocked our sense of safety to the nub, the real estate craze that followed a few years later gave us a reason to wager that the very notion of security, at least the kind made of four walls and a roof, was something that could be purchased, often without good credit or a down payment.

As caught up in all this static as I was, none of these factors had much to do with the reason I depleted most of my savings to buy a nine-hundred-square-foot bungalow for more than four times the money my parents had paid for the two-story, four-bedroom house I grew up in. At the time, I might have said otherwise. I probably insisted (I say "probably" since, as with all major life decisions, the relevant details tend to get lost in the mix; I do, however, remember the outfit I was wearing—a tank top with a strange and rather awful floral-patterned skirt—when I signed the escrow papers) that I was making an investment, that I was "putting my money in the safest place," that I was tired of dealing with landlords. All of that was true, but it was only years later that I could see there was something else going on entirely. I bought the house because I was thirty-four years old, had been self-employed most of my adult life, had never been married, was childless, had no boyfriend nor any appealing prospects in that department, and was hungry to the point of weakness for something that would root me to the earth.

Of course, that's as good a list as any of reasons *not* to buy a house. Freelance writers haven't historically been the best risks for mortgage lenders, and the absence of a romantic life, be it by choice, circumstance, or a narcissistic refusal to participate in Internet dating (which I suppose counted as a choice), doesn't on the surface seem relevant to the acquisition of property. But most people have a hard time separating the self from the home, and I was no exception. More than just shelter for ourselves and for our loved ones, more than just "the biggest purchase you'll ever make," a house is a repository for every piece of baggage we've ever carried. Our homes protect us from the outside world, show off our taste, and accommodate our stuff. Perhaps above all, they prove to ourselves and to the world that we've really and truly moved out of our childhood bedrooms.

But what do we do when a house makes life impossible? What if it threatens to destroy us? What do we do when the market tanks, the hillside collapses, the sub-prime mortgage comes home to roost, or we're just too tired to keep working the extra jobs and overtime now required to afford what used to be a staple of middle-class life? Do we stick it out? Do we cash out? Do we return to the life of a renter, with its aura of tapestry-covered, grad-student-style impermanence? Does selling your house mean losing your independence or gaining it? Does giving it up mean giving up on yourself?

Mercifully, I'm not losing my house to the bank. I have an old-fashioned thirty-year mortgage, and I make my payment every month. And despite the stucco incident, the property has hardly fallen into disrepair. It's true that at times home ownership has felt like a bigger burden than I imagined even in my most nail-biting pre-purchase moments. It's true that the money I've spent on plumbers and electricians and roofers and tree trimmers might ultimately have been put to better use on Hawaiian vacations while I remained an innocent renter. But the truth is that it wouldn't have really mattered. The cash would have slipped through my fingers anyway. Over the years, I've put preposterous amounts of energy and money into the places I've lived, even rentals. I've also put preposterous amounts into moving, storage, lost security deposits, and gas money for drives halfway across the country and back as I tried to figure out exactly where and how I wanted to live and whether my fitful bursts of house lust would ever translate into something approximating "settling down."

But this book is not just the story of the house I bought. It's also not just the story of other houses I tried to buy or of the disorienting yet sometimes hilarious effects of having a mother who seemed to rearrange the furniture more often than she changed her clothes. And while I could easily embark on a blow-by-blow of repairs and improvements and zombielike trips to Home Depot, while I could rehash every detail of faulty wiring or of ornery workmen or rats that feasted on the orange tree in the backyard, I'm going to try to keep a lid on that particular pot. That's the standard stuff of home-buying stories, and having now devoured more home repair manuals and sybaritic shelter magazines than the sum total of my college reading, I've come to think it's about as interesting as people recounting their dreams over the breakfast table.

Instead, this is the story of what happens when, for whatever reason, your identity becomes almost totally wrapped up not in who you are or how you live but in where you live. It's the story of how I came to care more about owning a house than committing to a partner or doing my job or even the ostensibly obvious fact that the sun would rise and set regardless of whether my name was on a mortgage. And though I can't presume to be able to shed new light on what, in precredit-crunch days, possessed vast numbers of Americans to ignore all logic and purchase houses they couldn't begin to afford, I do think we were all touched by the same strain of crazy. I may make my payments, but I suspect there isn't a terribly wide gulf between people whose houses have been repossessed and people who, like me, simply seem possessed by whatever version of grown-up life we were hoping to play out by playing house. This is the story of my lifelong game of house.

ONE

The first house I ever had fantasies about was a wood-and-glass octagon occupied by an imaginary person whose name I'd decided was Malcolm Apricot Dingo. The way I remember it, the house (which was real) looked more like a giant lemonade pitcher than a place where people might actually live. It sat on a weedy plot of land on a winding street, a tall, barrel-like structure that at certain times of day and given a certain arrangement of the window shades provided a view all the way through to the backyard. I was six years old, and this was a source of unending delight; the house made me feel as if I had X-ray vision, as if I were bionic.

Twice a day, my mother drove me past this house on our twenty-minute drive to and from my school. The commute had been made necessary by our recent move to a new neighborhood and my mother's last-minute decision, amid my begging and tears, to allow me to attend first grade at the same school where I'd attended kindergarten. The summer before, my parents had bought their first house, a yellow brick bungalow in a state of nearly unfathomable decay, and for all of my mother's enthusiasm about the new neighborhood she hadn't taken the final step of forcing me to attend school in the proper district. In retrospect, this deferment of the inevitable seems by turns tender and useless. I'd transfer to my zone-appropriate school the following year. The year after that, we'd pack our belongings in a rented Ryder truck and move seventeen hundred miles to yet another town and another school, where I'd stay for three years before another local move necessitated another clumsy navigation through a brine of strangers.

But in the year of the octagonal house, in those ten months when I passed it twice daily, each time announcing to my mother (I have an explicit memory of this, though she only vaguely recalls it) that Malcolm Apricot Dingo was watching us from behind the glass of what I was sure was his second-floor study, that having glanced up momentarily from his very important work he was waving to us, and that it was only polite that we wave back, I knew nothing of the gut-rattling chaos of being the new kid in school. I knew nothing of eating lunch alone while gamely pretending to read a book, of the indelibly bad impression that can be made from wearing the wrong clothes on the first day of school, of trying to forge friendships with people who've had the same best friend since before even the last time you were the new kid.

I also had little territorial frame of reference other than the lush, heat-stroked hill country of Austin, Texas, where we'd moved when I was three and where we'd stay until I was nearly nine. Though I was born in Palo Alto, California, and had trace memories of suburban Chicago, where my family had done a six-month stint when I was a toddler, the bulk of my early childhood was pure Texan. I had a drawl; I said "y'all" and "ahs cream" and assumed that everyone else in the world did, too. I also assumed that every summer day everywhere topped out at 108 degrees and that all cockroaches were the size of turtles and that armadillos were a common form of roadkill. My brother, who was four years younger than I, had been born in Austin in 1974, making him a native Texan. The retired couple who lived next door and whose college-aged children I worshipped were like surrogate grandparents. The city was also home to my friends, my babysitters, my school, my cat—in other words, everything that mattered. I was blond and perpetually tanned and pocked with bites from Texas mosquitoes.

I also happened to have an almost alarming fixation on *Little House on the Prairie* (first the TV show and, as soon as I could read, the books). I wore a sunbonnet passed down from my maternal great-grandmother, kept my hair in braids like Laura Ingalls, and occasionally called my parents Ma and Pa. When the bonnet wore down to a rag, my mother got out her sewing machine, which she often used to make our clothes, and whipped up a new one. At my request, she also helped me put my mattress on top of two box springs and leaned a stepladder against it, thereby mimicking the loft-bed setup of the Ingalls girls. In the yellow brick bungalow, where my mother built an elevated wooden play structure among the pecan trees in the backyard, I wore my bonnet along with an odd, scratchy calico skirt (a garment that could only have existed in the mid-1970s) and reenacted all manner of scenes from the books and TV episodes: the barn burning down, the dog getting lost, the whole family nearly dying from scarlet fever.

One day, my mother came to me and said that we would be moving away to New Jersey. I remember sobbing in her arms but also taking comfort in her promise that there would be snow in the new place. Since there was snow in the *Little House on the Prairie* books, I figured we were moving closer to the frontier. When she told me there'd be a real wood-burning fireplace in the new house, I imagined us using it for cooking corn bread.

Ridgewood, New Jersey, was no frontier, just a leafy village of perfectly clipped lawns abutting perfectly maintained houses. Mothers there did not sew clothes, much less build backyard play structures. In fact, they appeared not to do much of anything except play tennis, a discovery that seemed to turn my mother, who'd spent her Austin days attending Equal Rights Amendment rallies in peasant skirts, into an unhappy person almost overnight. Ironically, it was she who'd spearheaded the plan to move to Ridgewood. When my father, who'd been teaching music at the University of Texas, decided he wanted to live the life not of an academic but, rather, of a freelance composer (for commercial jingles, then hopefully for film and television) in New York, my mother had repeated the thing she'd apparently said shortly before they wed: "This marriage is about your career." She then sought relocation advice from our neighbors/surrogate grandparents, who, as it happened, had lived much of their lives in Ridgewood, New Jersey.

"It's a little pricier," they'd said. "But it's the best."

"I like it here," I said.

"Of course you do," my mother told me. "But if we stayed here, we wouldn't get to live in a new house!"

As I said, this book is about houses: ones I've lived in and ones I haven't, ones I've lusted for, ones I've reviled, ones I've left too soon, and ones where I've found myself stuck, chained to my own radiator by the tethers of my own stupid decisions. But if there's anything I've learned over the many years and many moves, it's this: a house is not the same as a home. Despite certain Muzak-sounding catchphrases of the real estate world—"home buyer," "home sales," "home loans"—the words "house" and "home" are not interchangeable. You buy a house, but you make a home. You do not shop for a "home" any more than you'd shop for a life. And by way of explaining how easy it can be to lose track of these distinctions, I need to lay out a few things about the home I grew up in and the homes my parents came from before that.

I need first of all to say that we weren't unhappy. Not acutely and not most of the time. Instead, what characterized our little unit—my parents, my brother, and me—was a chronic, lulling sensation of being aboard a train that was perpetually two stops away from the destination we had in mind for ourselves. And while I have to emphasize that the reasons for that aren't ultimately related to moving—or even to the fact that we tended to talk about moving in the same salivating, should-we-or-shouldn't-we tones in which some families talk about far-flung ski trips—I don't think it's a stretch to say that our lack of enthusiasm for ourselves had a lot to do with our perpetual curiosity about what possibilities for happiness might lie at the destination point of a moving van. We weren't much for card games or sports, but we knew how to escape from places.

And if you're looking for examples of people who escaped their humble beginnings, my parents qualify. My mother was born in 1942 in Carbondale, Illinois, a coal-mining town that also happened to be a university town. Carbondale is near the southern tip of the state, a hundred miles southeast of St. Louis and two hundred miles north of Memphis. And due to a constellation of factors, not least of all having a difficult, childlike mother who was threatened to the point of hysterics by anything that hinted of intellectual ambition (my grandmother forced my mother to twirl a baton and forbade her to attend the university lab high school because it was "uppity"), my mother loathed anything associated with her hometown and its environs. While I was growing up, she invoked Carbondale as though offering an excuse. It was both a form of self-flagellation and a rationale for any perceived shortcoming. "Well, when you're from southern Illinois, you _____ (can't use chopsticks/have never been to Europe/aren't sure what Passover is/can't really get behind psychotherapy)." In a family that specialized in judgment and criticism, that quickly grew bored with all that was innocuous or inoffensive or even pleasant but loved to chew on grievances as though they were slabs of meat on the bone, southern Illinois was the original sin. All that my mother saw of it—at least all I ever perceived her to have seen—appeared to be stewing in its own backwater. And whether or not these were the actual truths of the place, whether or not this was really all there was, she cringed at and reviled it all: the hillbilly intonations of the regional accent, the limited cultural offerings of the community (dinner theater, Elks' Club polka), the deep-fried cuisine, the ubiquitous polyester clothing, the knee-jerk political leanings, the xenophobia, the poverty, the heat, the humidity, the tangy efflux of the hickory and crab apple trees themselves.

As a result, her life became devoted almost exclusively to the cause of being the opposite of these things, to being educated, well-spoken, with-it, and, above all, sophisticated—or at least the version of sophistication she imagined when she surveyed her home life and conjured a view 180 degrees in the other direction. Lacking the financial or familial support to leave town, my mother enrolled in the local university and began assembling the tools necessary for her eventual escape. She became an accomplished pianist. She learned how to speak with clarity and confidence. Perhaps most important (she's explained this herself; it's not just my conjecture), she dated a guy whose parents seemingly knew a thing or two about the world. Sure, they were from Carbondale, but their house had books and records. It also had *The New Yorker* magazine. On visits to their place, my mother would flip through the mysterious pages as though she were glimpsing a distant, dazzling land. And even though she turned down her suitor's marriage proposal because he was "ultimately dull," she never forgot the portal those magazine pages provided into a befuddling but obviously superior world. It wasn't so much that she wanted to live in New York—that would come later and with a vengeance—as that she wanted to live in a place that resembled the kind of place that a person who read *The New Yorker* would live.

Her primary means of expression for this ambition: houses. She wasn't blessed with a willowy body type that might otherwise have made fashion her canvas, nor did she have an aptitude for foreign languages or interest in travel that could have made her genuinely cosmopolitan (her younger brother, for his part, escaped the muck of their household by growing up to be an inveterate globetrotter). But she did know what to do with paint colors, with curtains, with furniture. In fact, she had more than a few shades of brilliance on that front. Despite having grown up in a nondescript one-story brick house with no art on the walls and no books on the shelves, she had her share of opinions, however vague, about the kind of art (not from Sears) and books (not dime-store paperbacks) that would line the perimeters of the homes of her future. And, like a musician who could play by ear, she had the ability to conjure a room in her head and re-create it in three dimensions.

Given her generation and resources and station in life, my mother believed the best context for such a lifestyle was affiliation with a university. Not that she wanted to be an academic herself; she wanted to be an academic wife. Though she's never really explained to me how this aim came into being, I can only presume she'd run into a few of these types while growing up and they'd made a positive impression on her. After all, Carbondale, though it wasn't Cambridge or even Lincoln, Nebraska (where, decades later, I would eventually flee when the ripple effect of my mother's dreams began to feel like a choke hold), was a university town. Despite the not insignificant poverty rate, it was also a place where, every night, someone in some house (maybe even a few people in a few houses) sat down to dinner with a glass of red wine and a Mozart sonata. And having glimpsed some version of this scene on one or two occasions (perhaps as a babysitter, perhaps for ten seconds while dropping off a paper at a professor's house), my mother decided she wanted nothing more but would settle for nothing less. Thus she kept her eyes peeled for someone whose cautious, noncommittal bohemianism would mesh with her own and, with any luck, help supply her with the ultimate proof that she had transcended her origins: an elegant yet understated house with floor-to-ceiling bookshelves, the perfunctory hardwood-floor/Oriental-rug combo, and a kitchen stocked with hanging copper pots and a copy of *The Moose-wood Cookbook.*

This was my mother's vision in the mid-1960s (minus the *Moosewood,* which didn't pub until 1977 but, even in the days before Woodstock, surely was a twinkle in the eyes of an entire generation of women). This was what she believed she wanted: not a career, not even the life of a genuine intellectual, but the trappings of that kind of life. She wanted the house, the rugs, the shelves. So was it blind faith my mother brought to the table the day she decided—and I have no doubt she was decisive in the matter; it's a skill I've always admired in her but didn't fully inherit—that my father was the train to which she was hitching her almost violent need to transform herself? Did she simply love him for the sake of loving him? Or did she look at him and catch some vision of an educated, well-spoken, and sophisticated life? Did she see in him some iteration of a *New Yorker* cartoon character (not beyond the realm of possibility, given his prominent nose and the mad-professor-style tufts of hair that flanked his already bald pate) and conclude via a series of unconscious calculations that of all the grad students in the music department of Southern Illinois University, he was the one most likely to help her succeed?

Two years her senior, my father was well-known to be a virtuosic composer and musical arranger and destined for a life of some variety of creative greatness. Still, if ever there was a case of raw, uncultivated, and by-all-appearances limitless musical gifts unsullied (that is, unassisted) by careerism of any kind, it was the case of my father, a man who would eventually leave academia to pursue a freelance career that was sometimes so fraught with paranoia and resentment that his own children would be forbidden to watch certain television programs because he'd been considered but not ultimately hired for the job of composing music for them. (Hint: I had not seen a complete episode of *The Simpsons* until my junior year of college.)

But in 1965 in Carbondale, concerns of this caliber were unimaginable. This was a world in which St. Louis was considered a glittering, faraway metropolis and wedding receptions took place in church basements over Hawaiian Punch. My mother says her wedding cost $200, and she likes to emphasize that at twenty-three, she was considered an old bride. She also tells me this: upon their engagement, my father's mother came to my mother and warned her against marrying her indolent, no-account son. Whereas my father's mother could see that her future daughter-in-law was ambitious and possessed (thanks undoubtedly to her efforts to define herself in opposition to her mother) of a keen sense of social protocol, she saw her son as aimless and uncensored, a beatnik who shot his mouth off without apology, a musical savant whose anachronistic tastes (Glenn Miller, Sarah Vaughan, no interest in Elvis Presley whatsoever) threatened to lend a freakish taint to what otherwise might have been an aura of cool. Whereas my mother was organized and a self-starter, my father was a weird dreamer. Whereas my mother was from a respectable family (her parents might have been lackluster, but her uncle was an ophthalmologist who lived in a two-story redbrick Colonial straight out of a Currier and Ives painting), my father's background, at least as far as I understood it, was a slightly milder version of Faulkner.

Not that my paternal grandmother, by then a holy-rolling evangelical who eschewed rock and roll and wouldn't have approved of Elvis anyway, put her son's deficits in quite these terms. But for all her whacked-out self-loathing, you can see where she was coming from. The poverty surrounding my father's upbringing has, at least to my coddled, suburban sensibilities, always stunned me to the point of nearly voyeuristic fascination. When I was a child, the salient detail of my father's upbringing, to me, involved the absence of indoor plumbing. His family had had an outhouse until he was twelve. Most mind-blowing of all, this wasn't a country outhouse in the nineteenth century like on *Little House on the Prairie* but an outhouse for a house in town. In the 1950s.

But wouldn't you know it: my father was also seduced by *The New Yorker*. As a high-school student, he would visit the library of his hometown of Centralia, Illinois, and read the jazz reviews of Whitney Balliett. He would learn about who was playing at the Village Vanguard. He would read descriptions of musicians, such as Bill Evans, he'd never heard but would later come to revere, and try to imagine what New York would be like in real life. Shortly after my parents married, my father did a brief stint as a fellow at the Eastman School of Music in Rochester, after which he and my mother drove down to New York City. They stayed in the Tudor Hotel on Forty-second Street and Second Avenue and went one night to the Village Vanguard. A friend of a friend from Eastman met them and then took my father to a bar where jazz musicians were known to hang out. There, my father saw many famous players, including some he'd read about in *The New Yorker*. Until then, he hadn't ever entirely comprehended the idea that people actually lived in New York. As spellbound as he was, he didn't consider staying. He was married, after all, and he and my mother both had teaching jobs waiting in Indiana.

As my mother frequently pointed out when I was growing up, she and my father had "come extraordinarily far." By this she meant that they'd pulled themselves further up the social and cultural ladder than could fairly be expected of anyone from southern Illinois, much less two people who'd been dealt such a difficult set of childhood conditions. They might not have made it to New York, but within four years of getting married, they found themselves in Palo Alto, where my father had been given an opportunity to earn a Ph.D. in music in exchange for writing arrangements for the Stanford marching band. I was born during that time, after which we made the aforementioned moves to the Chicago suburb and then to Austin, where, after nearly six years, we made that jolting move to New Jersey.

But let's stay in Palo Alto for a moment. From the time they'd arrived there, my parents not only began subscribing to *The New Yorker* but also managed to take on several other qualities they associated with the kinds of people my mother often referred to as "classy" and "high-powered." A few of these trappings had to do with things like speaking properly and driving European cars, even if that meant used, rusted Volkswagens. More of them, however, were expressed (with an enthusiasm that bordered on the obsessive) via houses and home decor. And since my own housing compulsions are a direct descendant of my mother's efforts to cope with the identity confusion that plagued our immediate family like a skin rash, I simply can't talk about where I've lived without explaining where my parents have lived. Literally and figuratively, their foundations were shakier than any seismic fault line.

But this instability was nothing that couldn't be remedied— or at least covered up in high style—by those hardwood floors and Oriental rugs. Inspired by the musty gravitas of certain professors' houses in Palo Alto, whose combination of old-money regality (tattered volumes of the *OED* on stands, yellowed maps of Nova Scotia) and flower power–inspired clutter (anything macramé) filled her with the promise of overcoming the yokelness of her upbringing, my mother modeled our houses on the image of her ideal self.

Moreover, she often did so on minuscule or even nonexistent budgets. In Austin, despite my father's unremarkable assistant professor salary, she managed to turn that dilapidated bungalow (the previous owner had lived in a single chair for something approaching fifteen years until he finally died, mountains of TV-dinner boxes and yellowed pages from the *Austin American-Statesman* blocking the light from the windows) into a veritable advertisement for the upper-middle-class, liberal elite. The white oak floors, delicately resanded and ritualistically doused with Pine-Sol, the intricately thought-out splashes of color (a sapphire blue wall in the archway between the living room and the dining room, an abstract mural in the kitchen), the built-in floor-to-ceiling bookshelves, the omnipresent jazz or classical music: to me, all of it meant home. But to my parents, especially my mother, who kept touching up that kitchen mural practically until the day we moved out (think swirls and circles in earth tones, Rothko meets lava lamp), all of it meant they'd escaped their old home.

Except something happened after we packed up and drove—my father in a rented Ryder truck, my mother in a Plymouth Horizon with me and my brother in the backseat and our cat in a wire mesh carrier—seventeen hundred miles to the place that would technically be our home for the duration of my childhood. As I've said, I wasn't yet nine. I can't reasonably suggest that the move bifurcated my childhood in any kind of measurable way. While I knew how to ride my bike to friends' houses in the immediate neighborhood and was sufficiently enmeshed in the terrain that I rarely passed a honeysuckle bush without grabbing a blossom and siphoning out the sap right then and there, I was not old enough to know the streets, to have memorized the skyline, to have forged friendships that had any real hallmarks of inseparability. I would never, of course, be from Austin, since I would spend the subsequent ten years—the bulk of my childhood and all of my adolescence—in Ridgewood, New Jersey. Ridgewood would be where I'd experience my first kiss, get my driver's license, and graduate from high school. In 2008 I would attend my twentieth high-school reunion, and it would be the banquet room of a Wyndham Garden Hotel in New Jersey that, at no small expense, I'd take planes and trains and taxis to reach. Once there, I'd greet my former classmates in a genuine spirit of nostalgia and shared history.

That said, I have never been able to say I'm from New Jersey without feeling as if I were wearing someone else's name tag at a party. For all the time I spent there, for all the ways in which my speech can tilt ever so subtly into the nasally timbre of a tristate mall queen (though, curiously and somewhat embarrassingly, those "y'all's" creep back into place when I'm in Texas), the place still feels to me like the wrong exit off a highway my parents weren't quite equipped to be driving on in the first place. This was due as much to the particular town as to the state. As out of place as we were in New Jersey as a whole (there's practically nothing about the boisterousness and raggedy mirth of a typical Jerseyite that would appear to share any DNA with the members of my own gene pool), we managed to pick a town that reduced us to a late-1970s version of the Beverly hillbillies.

And that's not just because we pulled in to town in that Ryder truck and, thanks to a minor accident, a freshly dented Plymouth Horizon. It's because we essentially had no business being there. Whereas most of the dads were Wall Street brokers and corporate executives and doctors, my dad was an aspiring writer of commercial jingles (he was going to move on to bigger things, yes, but first he needed to feed his family). Whereas most of the moms, as I mentioned, played tennis, my mom played Brahms on the piano and continued to fume about the nonpassage of the Equal Rights Amendment.

Whereas most of the kids wore ski parkas proudly adorned with lift tickets, I had never really seen snow.

You would think that moving from Austin, Texas, to Ridgewood, New Jersey—locales that despite certain cultural differences shared a common language, maintained similar standards of health and hygiene, and both used the English system of measurement—wouldn't exactly be tantamount to immigrating to a foreign land. But somehow for us it was. A markedly desirable town thanks to its proximity to New York City and to its good public schools, Ridgewood was also a markedly uptight town, at least compared to the languorous hippiedom of Austin. Not only could my parents not understand why my playmates' mothers wanted to be called Mrs. —— rather than by their first names, but they literally could not understand what people were saying. En route to New Jersey during the move, after our Plymouth Horizon was sideswiped by an 18-wheel tractor trailer just after crossing the state line on I-95, my mother was reduced to near tears when a state trooper's recommendations for taking surface streets the rest of the way involved "da toyd cycle." It was only after drawing a map on the back of a Burger King bag ("sack" in our red state parlance) that it became clear he was talking about a series of traffic circles and some significance involving the third one: "toyd cycle" translated to "third circle." By then, it hardly mattered anymore. We were less than a mile inside New Jersey borders, and we were already in the seventh cycle of hell.

Maybe that's overstating things. We did, to my wide-eyed delight, receive a visit from a representative from the Ridgewood Welcome Wagon, a Florence Henderson look-alike who showered us with a fruit basket and coupons for discounted dry cleaning and free desserts at Friendly's. But I think I can also safely say that on just about every level, the social currency that circulated among upper-middle-class mid-Atlantic-state residents rendered the dollar value of my parents' Midwestern-bred, academic-influenced lifestyle nearly worthless. Despite the townspeople's fixations on being able to put elite college stickers on the backs of their station wagons, my parents had no real concept of the power of networks formed through these institutions. They had never traveled abroad. The term "summerhouse" was alien to them. Whereas other families vacationed on Sanibel Island or Cape Cod, our out-of-town getaways usually involved driving to southern Illinois. We did not, I now suspect, have quite enough money even for that. As it was, we didn't have health insurance for the first few years.

The result of all this dissonance was a certain unacknowledged chaos, self-doubt disguised as superiority, joylessness masquerading as something my mother might have called "serious-mindedness." And in an often frantic-seeming effort to cope, we made two-facedness our family crest. Out in the world, we pretended to be proud and happy citizens of northern New Jersey. I took jazz and tap-dancing lessons twice a week. My brother mounted lemonade stands in the front yard. My father took me to the bakery on Sunday mornings to buy donuts, and my mother shopped in the downtown dress shops and stood in line at Rite Aid like any other mother. But within the confines of the house, all niceties and efforts at respectable suburban conduct were checked at the door. Arriving home from school, I'd launch into a theatrical diatribe about how terrible my day had been (it rarely was truly terrible, but somehow the rants were cathartic), how intolerable my teacher and classmates were, how beneath my dignity it was that we'd had to play dodgeball/draw triangles/set the Pledge of Allegiance to music. In response, my mother would often say something like "Well, if you think —— is a nitwit, you should meet her mother." Later, at the dinner table, withering critiques of friends and neighbors—"he thinks Bach is pronounced 'Batch'!"—were not only tolerated but encouraged.

As snobby as we were, we were hardly polymaths. My father's opinions were almost exclusively confined to matters of music; my mother's extended to music and home decor. Looking back, I wonder if some other family was sitting around their dinner table saying, "The Daums don't even have passports, can you *imagine*?" But at the time, our shared disdain for our surroundings seemed as integral to those surroundings as the trees and sidewalks themselves. We complained, therefore we were. We excoriated the town, therefore it was home.

Did it have to be like this? Could we have taken another tack? Was it possible that with a different approach, we could have found an antidote for this particular form of overprivileged, underintellectual (not *anti*-intellectual; most Ridgewoodians weren't so much opposed to the life of the mind as they were just generally more interested in the stock market), oxford-shirt-wearing, weekend-golfing, leaf-blowers-blaring-at-7:00-a.m. boorishness? Is there any way we could have taken all that fractiousness and converted it into something useful?

In theory, we could have moved to New York City. We could have skipped Ridgewood entirely and driven the Ryder truck out of Texas and up the eastern seaboard and straight over the George Washington Bridge. We also could have wised up after a year or so in the burbs and shifted the contents of our rented Tudor house to some railroad apartment on the Upper West Side, where my mother would be freed from starchy PTA moms and presumably kids would know how to pronounce "Bach." In theory we could have done this, but in theory we could also have become missionaries in Malawi. In practice it was never going to happen. For all the courage and energy my parents had mustered in forging a route from southern Illinois to their various destinations, New York City required a faster metabolism than either of them could have hoped to achieve. Plus, for all their disdain of suburban prissiness, they found themselves reluctantly in agreement with Ridgewoodians on at least one point: the city was no place to raise kids.

My parents were obsessed with New York—its mythologies, its towering density, its promise of high-powered talent pools and professional opportunities. But they were also cowed by it, and understandably so. In the late 1970s and early 1980s it was dangerous and dirty and, given the way the squalid, hooker-filled Port Authority Bus Terminal book-ended just about every one of our trips in from New Jersey, just ever so slightly third world in its ambience. My father was once mugged at knife-point; another time a small girl romping down a Hell's Kitchen street errantly threw a piece of metal shrapnel in his direction. It hit him in the face and caused profuse bleeding; the girl ran away, terrified. This was the era of the removable car radio, and whenever we drove into the city, my father would pop out the cassette deck and hand it to my mother to carry in her purse.

Still, my father often spoke of the perils of New York, particularly the West Side midtown neighborhoods where he was attempting to do business, with a certain relish, almost as though he were bragging.

"Well, New York is great, but it's not quite civilized," I'd hear him say on the phone to friends in faraway places who we all imagined were marveling at the scope of our ambition.

"There's a sense of lawlessness. The city will eat you alive. I can see how a lot of people just wouldn't be able to handle it."

Both of my parents, my mother especially, were fond of suggesting to various Midwestern and Texan friends and relatives that we actually lived not in New Jersey but, rather, in some kind of staging area between the vacuous suburbs and the head rush of Gotham.

"Yes, the address says New Jersey," my mother would say. "But we're just right over the border from Manhattan. Just right there. Very close."

This was not true. We were completely and utterly in New Jersey. We were twenty miles away, and it was a long twenty miles, psychologically if not geographically. Still, as though standing at the western mouth of the Lincoln Tunnel and trying to see a sliver of light from the other side, my parents peered at their dream lives from afar and did everything they could to convince themselves that they were wide awake and living them. This effort was aided somewhat by the fact that my father did much of his work out of Chicago, which had a thriving jingle-writing scene and where he had a number of professional connections dating back to his graduate school days. Why we hadn't just moved to Chicago I wasn't sure, but I remember my mother repeatedly saying that my father "had to be known as a New York guy in order to get hired by the Chicago guys." For at least the first five years that we were in Ridgewood, my father was in Chicago more often than he was not. And though that put my mother in the somewhat awkward position of appearing to be a single parent even though she wasn't, she would later tell me that his absences were among the few respites from what otherwise amounted to a life of relentless if weirdly indescribable stress.

On weeks when my father was home, he'd go into New York

and, as he put it, "hustle for work." I'm pretty sure that no one, let alone him, entirely understood what this needed to entail (he didn't have an agent or a rep and to this day has never felt he needed one), but my perception was that he functioned as something like a traveling salesman for himself. He dropped off his demo tape to music production companies and ad agencies. He had lunch with people who, presumably, were in a position to hire him. He was assaulted by little girls and mugged. Mostly it seemed, however, that he walked around the city, particularly the seedy midtown neighborhoods on the West Side that housed various recording studios and the musicians' union and restaurants frequented by players in pit orchestras of Broadway shows. And amid all this pavement pounding, his unconscious disbelief that he'd actually made it that far out of Centralia, Illinois, became the collective unconscious of the family.

"I was just there!" my father would exclaim whenever a Manhattan landmark appeared on television. "Walked down that street just today. That's Broadway and, looks like, Fifty-fourth Street. No, Fifty-fifth. I was just there. Had my meeting on Fifty-seventh Street and walked south to the Port Authority. Yes, I know exactly where that is. Know it well."

We went through two houses in Ridgewood, the small rented Tudor and, later, a slightly larger house built in 1931 in the American Foursquare style on a street I'll call Jones Lane. In each of these houses my parents maintained two telephone lines: one for normal, family-related matters and one called "the business line," which was designated for my father's work and was never to be picked up by children. (Once or twice my mother answered and impersonated a professional receptionist.) An answering machine (a technological marvel) hooked up to the business line delivered an authoritative message designed to give the caller the impression that this was no house in suburbia but, rather, a bona fide professional operation.

Two separate phone lines was an exotic household feature in 1979. More exotic still was the ability to retrieve messages from remote locations using a small beeper that emitted a tone that would rewind and play the tape. I don't know if this feature preceded the technology wherein you checked messages by simply pressing a phone-pad key or if my parents—likely my father—had chosen this particular model out of some belief that it was superior to the more conventional system (we were a Betamax family, so that should tell you something). But I remember clearly that the beeper, which was activated by a push button that had no lock, would sputter out electronic hisses as it got tossed around in my mother's oversized purse. As a result, when she walked around, she often gave the impression of being attached to some kind of homing device. Once she sat her purse down on a supermarket checkout counter only to have the beeper emit a solid, unrelenting tone that, in her efforts to dig it out of her bag, caused her to spill the entire contents onto the conveyor belt and the floor. I remember being terrified that she was going to explode into a rage. I remember that I was sheepishly holding a candy bar that I was about to implore her to buy and that the clerk, a high-school student with fashionably feathered-back hair and a gold cross around her neck, looked at us as though we'd accidentally wandered into the store from some faraway land of disheveled women carrying strange technological gadgets. That is to say, she looked at us in confusion and, as far as I was concerned, disdain.

Justifiably or not (probably not, but what does it matter?), this was how I experienced just about everything about life in

Ridgewood, New Jersey, particularly in the first few years after our arrival. Even when I was as young as nine, I had the sense that everyone there already knew each other, that every clique was already formed, that everyone's mom knew all the other moms, that maybe there were even secret underground tunnels connecting the houses so that entire social networks could thrive without my even knowing they existed. And watching the checkout girl watching my mother pick the contents of her purse off the floor, I remember feeling so diminished by what I perceived to be her total, inviolable sense of belonging and our total, inviolable sense of otherness that I wanted to disappear, beeper in hand, into the far reaches of the frozen food cases and cryogenically preserve myself until I was older and could flee the town forever.

But the beeper was hardy the final frontier in our telecommunication adventures. More astonishing was that the business line had two numbers associated with it: a New Jersey number and a Manhattan number with a 212 area code. The line operated on a call-forwarding system, which meant that once you programmed it by dialing in a set of codes, calls to the Manhattan number would ring through automatically to the New Jersey number. Each line had its own similar but distinct version of the old-fashioned Ma Bell ring tone, and in the early Ridgewood years the jangle of the business line sent an almost bone-cracking jolt of nervous energy through the house.

"It's the business line! Dad, the business line is ringing!" my brother and I would yell, terrified that one of us would pick up the phone by accident and also terrified that one of our parents wouldn't get to it in time. "Dad, get it! Dad, it's business!"

Somehow my parents had cobbled together the money to

rent a musty one-room office in a shabby building on Fortieth Street and Ninth Avenue. This was not only home to a desk and filing cabinets and an Oriental rug my mother had placed strategically over the industrial carpet but also the official headquarters of the business line. Though it was generally unclear what actually took place in this office (my father's keyboards and reel-to-reel tape recorders, which were crucial to his creative process, were permanently installed at home), the intended effect was to cover up—or at least distract from—the fact that we lived in New Jersey. Business cards and stationery bearing the Manhattan address were printed. A small sofa and a ficus plant were installed in the corner so that my father could take meetings with clients.

Though I'm sure a few meetings did occur, what I remember most about the office in Manhattan is how little time my father actually spent there. As for the business line, not only did it not ring with the frequency my parents had hoped, but it had the unfortunate glitch of being forwardable only if you happened to be physically using the phone from which you wished to forward calls. That detail sticks in my mind thanks to the memory of one occasion wherein my father returned home from a day of "hustling" and making and taking a few calls in the office only to realize that he'd forgotten to reset the business line so that it would ring through to the house in New Jersey.

"Oh, hell," my mother said. She had already started dinner.

"Well, is anyone really going to call?" my father asked.

"Possibly," my mother said, alluding to this music supervisor or that Broadway show producer (my mother really wanted my father to write music for Broadway shows).

"You're saying I should go back?" he said. It was rush hour. It was a Friday. Thanks to heavy traffic, my father's journey on the Short Line bus from the Port Authority to the drop-off location at the Kmart on Route 17 had taken nearly an hour.

"Don't you think you should?" my mother said with exasperation if not unkindness. "Otherwise we're talking about a whole weekend of calls not able to come through."

So my father got in the Plymouth Horizon and drove back into the city, found a parking spot several blocks from his destination, walked to the office, reprogrammed the phone, and drove back to Ridgewood. Meanwhile, we ate dinner without him. The business line didn't ring that weekend.

And so went life in New Jersey, a place that was at once too rich for our blood and too uncool to ever truly own up to. When we traveled to Chicago to join my father, I'd once again watch in befuddled silence as my mother told his colleagues we were from New York. When my father's mother and then my mother's father died the two consecutive years following our arrival in Ridgewood and we had to make trips to southern Illinois, I more than once overheard my mother implying to various relatives—the kind unlikely to pull out a map and figure out anything to the contrary—that we lived "in the city."

Should my parents have abandoned their caution and moved to Manhattan anyway, tucking themselves into the bristly folds of urban bohemia until they either made it or could return home with the satisfaction of having tried? Should my brother and I have been made to brave the menaces of the New York City schools? Would my mother, so angry for so many years in Ridgewood, have been better off being angry at muggers and car radio thieves than at suburban tennis ladies? Would she have been angry at all? Could my parents have cured their obsession with New York by simply giving in to it? Could they have sidestepped the insecurity that begat the phoniness that begat the chronic sense of estrangement and made themselves into genuine New Yorkers the old-fashioned way, by faking it for as long as it took to start truly making it?

Of course they should have. It's just that they should have done it all twenty years earlier, minus the kids and probably minus each other. My father, bless his uncensored and cranky soul, has in moments admitted as much. Now that his children are grown, he's glad he had them, he's told me, but it probably wasn't the ideal trajectory for his life. My mother, because she is a mother, would never say such a thing, not least of all because she'd never think it. As much as she wanted a ticket out of her hometown and state, I'm pretty sure she wanted a family even more, and as much as it breaks my heart to contemplate it, the idea that you could flee to the big city to pursue a career and *then* have a family was probably beyond the imaginative powers of most twenty-three-year-old southern Illinois women in 1965. Besides, for all their bold life maneuvers, neither she nor my father—individually or together—would have been brazen enough to catch the Greyhound bus out of town back when they probably should have. True to Midwestern form, they believed in being prepared, in waiting their turn, in not going off half-cocked. And so their time in Ridgewood went from two years to four years to fifteen years. My father finally found some success and started making some money (twice, he won Emmy Awards for music he'd written for a cartoon program; this one we were allowed to watch). My mother finally found a career and, thus, a little happiness. We didn't move to New York City, nor did we move to Connecticut, Westchester County, or another part of New Jersey. This was surprising only insofar as, until I was in junior high school, we spent most weekends in these places looking at houses.

We were a family without hobbies. We did not ski, hike, or participate in team sports. We did not play board games or cards. There was music, of course, but it was a despotic passion that doubled as a vocation and therefore did not count as a recreational activity. Instead, if there was anything that came close to a regular weekend activity, it was attending open houses. My mother, who was devouring shelter magazines before they became the wallpaper of the nation itself, often seemed physically unable to restrain herself from looking at an interesting house she'd seen listed in the newspaper. Sometimes these houses were down the block; sometimes they were in other states—and when she brought me along, it was as if she were dangling a new life in front of me. In the sixth grade, a year in which I was particularly miserable thanks to yet another school change when we moved across town to Jones Lane, I remember my mother becoming fascinated by the town of Westport, Connecticut, a high-WASP hamlet on the shores of Long Island Sound. We went there three or four weekends in a row, enlisting the help of a Realtor who showed us a handful of vaguely run-down properties surrounded by marshy grasses and ferns. And although my father, when he went at all, was solely along for the ride and appeared to have no interest in moving, it didn't take long for me to decide I desperately wanted to move there. With the recent school transfer, I'd made some minor efforts to remake myself, mainly by announcing that I wanted to be known not as Meghan but as Meg. And with that choice no longer sitting well, not to mention my discovery that you were nothing in this school if you weren't a cheerleader for Ridgewood's version of the Pop Warner football team (an enterprise denigrated by my parents, who forbade me to try out for cheerleading), the prospect of a do-over was appealing. My mother had somehow developed the idea that Westport, whose fusty, old-money New England–ness contrasted with Ridgewood's slightly nouveau-riche glitz, was an "intellectual" place. There was an appealing bookstore, a regional theater, and concerts in the park. In turn, I figured that maybe the cheerleaders were a bit brainier and might therefore be acceptable to my parents. I wondered if it would be like my first (seemingly more academically minded) school in Ridgewood or, better yet, like Austin, where my babysitters had not been surly teenagers but grad students who wore dashikis and the world had not seemed like a place you had to wipe your feet before walking around in.

Obviously, my perceptions were monumentally, laughably off. Westport was and is one of the wealthiest towns in the United States: a cradle of privilege and preppiness, not to mention the setting of *The Man in the Gray Flannel Suit*. We would have been more out of place there than we were even in Ridgewood. We didn't move. We couldn't have even begun to afford it—I can't imagine what made my mother think otherwise—and besides, they'd bought the house on Jones Lane less than a year earlier. It was also considerably farther away from New York City than Ridgewood—fifty miles rather than twenty—which would have made emergency trips to reset the business line even more tedious than they already were. I have a specific memory of standing in one house in Westport, a shabby split-level that my mother would never have even considered in Ridgewood, and hearing my father ask the Realtor if New York City radio stations, such as NPR's Manhattan affiliate or the jazz station out of Columbia University, came in up there. The Realtor said she didn't think so. Sometime not long after, the subject of Westport was dropped.

Instead of moving, my mother put her domestic energies over the next six years into overseeing remodeling projects in the Jones Lane house. Though there were only four of us, we were a family that needed lots of rooms. We yelled a lot, talked on the phone at unnecessarily high volumes, and, for reasons ranging from the practical to the slightly pathetic (music practice in the living room was encouraged over after-school sports, weekend teenage socializing was frowned on if not officially forbidden), were simply home more often than we were out in the world. We needed doors that closed (and slammed) and hallways that drew clear lines between territories. Our houses over the years weren't large—we never had more than one bathroom—but no one could have accused us of not using every inch of space. By the time I was a senior in high school, my mother had spearheaded remodels of both the attic and the basement, projects that effectively gave each family member his or her own floor.

As it turned out, my mother needed much more than her own story. Having spent much of her time in Ridgewood trying unsuccessfully to find a professional niche for herself—she gave private piano lessons, wrote a libretto for a kids' musical, and, possessed of a pleasant, accent-free voice, attempted to become a voice-over artist by making a demo tape wherein she read magazine ad copy—she finally began to find her way shortly after I entered high school. Unfortunately for me, this involved essentially following me to high school. Here, my mother managed to finally shirk her self-appointed responsibilities as my father's de facto publicist/manager/personal assistant and transform herself into something she (and certainly we) never imagined she'd be: a theater person. Ridgewood had an established summer-stock program, in which I, having spent much of my childhood belting out tunes from the musical *Annie* in the hope of one day auditioning for the real show (I surpassed the height cutoff before this could happen), had enthusiastically enrolled. And what began as my mother volunteering her piano-playing services for productions of shows like *Carousel* and *Pippin,* where I ambled around in the chorus, grew into larger responsibilities: assistant music director, music director, producer, theater arts teacher.

My mother was tenured and then promoted several times. By the time I was in college, she was on her way to becoming something of the grande dame of the school's drama community (whereas she had once deplored the obstreperous carryings-on of teenagers, she was now the cool teacher who joined their fun). Needless to say, this journey was as positive and necessary and healthy for her as it was sometimes exasperating and cringe inducing for me. Equally needless to say (though I'll say it anyway, maybe out of some need to repeat the obvious to myself) is that she meant no harm. But if my late adolescence and early twenties were marked by any single experience, it was the experience of watching my mother transform her personality—and with it her style of dress, her speech mannerisms, and her taste in friends—in what seemed like less time than it took to mount a student production of *Godspell.* Seemingly overnight, she had traded her tone of abiding anger for a tone of abiding drama, her peasant blouses for colorful scarves and modernist jewelry, and, most notably, her residency on Jones Lane for the thing she hadn't realized she'd wanted all along: a house of her own.

The summer between my junior and my senior years of college, my mother moved out of Jones Lane and rented a small, cottagelike house in an adjacent town. After nearly twenty-five years of living with my father's moodiness and constant mono- logue of criticism, she had decided that the cure for her misery was not only a life in the student theater but also four walls whose color scheme required approval from no one. It wasn't another man she wanted but another life, preferably one in which she could drink wine in her sun-drenched living room and listen to George Winston CDs with no one ranting about the music being jejune and look at the art on her walls without feeling guilty that the other occupants of the house hated it. So one July day, movers came and transferred certain carefully selected pieces of furniture from our house to my mother's bachelorette pad less than ten miles away. The proceedings, I'm told, were not hostile but rather so infused with guilt and unaccepted apologies that my mother developed a rash on her neck from rubbing it in anxiety. From what I gathered, my father and brother simply sat there, swatting away mosquitoes in a nonplussed stupor.

By the time I deigned to get on the bus and travel the twenty miles from Manhattan, where I was living in squalid postadolescent rebellion in Greenwich Village, my mother's new house looked like a page from the (then quite au courant) Pottery Barn catalog. Sleek modernist pieces were flawlessly juxtaposed with antiques, cut flowers leaped from glazed ceramic vases, the framed art posters that had festooned the old house seemed now to have multiplied; between the plac- ards for my mother's theater productions and the original, mostly abstract art either sold by or created by her new friends, there was scarcely an inch of blank wall space. Too broke to buy significant pieces of new furniture and too chari- table to abscond with any major stuff from the old house, my mother had a living room sofa and chairs made of wicker. Though I do not remember this incident well (I suspect—make that hope—my mother remembers it hardly at all), I know she led me through the five rooms of the house with enough trepidation to suggest the parent-child relationship had been abruptly reversed.

"It's cute," I said.

This was a terrible time in my life. I was unhappy at college, and the unhappiness was exacerbated by guilt about being unhappy; it just seemed utterly inappropriate to the occasion. Depending on whom I was with (my mother being one example), I could be a real drag and this day was a case in point. I remember skulking around the house and eye-rollingly pronouncing it "nice" and "fine." I remember sitting outside on the patio and eating a meal of tomatoes, French bread, and polenta, a product my mother squeezed directly from its plastic, sausagelike packing onto an earthenware plate. I remember feeling that she wanted to have some kind of seminal mother-daughter conversation but was still too shell-shocked to dare to initiate one, a vulnerability I took full advantage of by retreating into near silence. I remember that I later realized that the wicker furniture in the living room was actually the porch furniture, recushioned, from the Jones Lane veranda.

Speaking of which, the Jones Lane house had developed the half-ghoulish, half-comical appearance of a refrigerator that's been raided by someone hoping to go unnoticed. Like tubs of ice cream furtively poked by stray fingers in the middle of the night, the rooms hadn't been emptied as much as they'd been manhandled into a patchier version of themselves. The sofa and dining table and the better armchairs still in place, it was smaller items—desk lamps, cheap bookshelves, a butcher board chopping block—that would suddenly reveal themselves as not there. You'd try to set down a glass of water while watching TV and realize the end table was missing. Kitchen supplies would be thinned out in a way that, oddly, was both insignificant and highly irritating; the flour sifter would be gone from the cupboard, the preferred salad tongs absent, the "good napkins" no longer folded in the drawer on top of the less good ones.

My mother has said that the initial idea behind getting her own house was that it would be a temporary arrangement. She simply wanted to see what living alone was like, to know she could do it, to check it off the list of life experiences that— by virtue of her generation or her hometown or her own choices—had heretofore been denied her. Indeed, in the beginning her house seemed very much like a young person's sublet. The small things that had been purloined from Jones Lane were my mother's big things. A single desk lamp would light her entire bedroom; an end table functioned as her desk. But given that unlike my father she had a regular salary and, what's more, that salary actually increased over time, it wasn't long before her house was properly outfitted and her suppos-edly temporary experiment in independent living graduated into permanence. She moved from the cottage-style house to a slightly larger, slightly more modern ranch-style house (a strange if vastly updated reimagining of the rented ranch house in Austin). A few years later, she bought the left-hand unit of a Tudor-style duplex near the Ridgewood train station.

The money for the duplex came from selling the Jones Lane house, an event that precipitated my father, partly at my urging, finally doing the thing he should have done in 1964: moving to New York City. There he lived—and continues to live—alone in a one-bedroom apartment near the Tudor Hotel whose living room was taken up almost entirely with music production equipment. There he was allowed to occupy all corners of his eccentricity. His inherent nocturnalism, which had always been cramped by family life and, even after my brother and I were gone, the noisy lawn mowers and early-closing restaurants of Ridgewood, was now tucked into the cradle of the never-sleeping city. As though the nonurban world had been a fifty-five-year nightmare from which he finally awoke, he seemed to forget about grassy terrain altogether, once complaining to me that he'd taken the bus all the way out to New Jersey to attend a Fourth of July barbecue only to find that it was, to his great distress, outdoors. Living in New York, he told me, made him "as content as I've ever been." Since he'd never been a believer in happiness (when I was in the seventh grade, he'd explained happiness to me as "something that exists purely in the past tense"), I saw this as a major accomplishment.

Years pass. Nearly ten. My mother lives happily in her Tudor-style duplex, a *House and Garden*–worthy abode exploding with color and art and flowers and light streaming through the sunroom windows and Sondheim music streaming through the Bose stereo. She has remade herself. She is a busy, animated, unattached woman with busy, animated friends and tickets to concerts and paintings made by artists she knows. She drives a pristine, preowned Alfa Romeo sedan that she bought from a gay male friend for what she claims was not an inordinate amount of money. When she orders a drink, she asks for an Absolut gimlet on the rocks. When she goes on vacation, it's to Vermont and to "the Cape." Her son has gone to college in California and never returned back east. Her daughter has moved more times than it seems possible to count. Her husband is still legally her husband, partly for health insurance reasons (thanks to self-employment and heart disease, he cannot get his own) and partly because their apparently mutual love of solitude has precluded the burgeoning of any new relationships that prove significant enough to necessitate a divorce. Ultimately, they will live apart—and alone—for longer than they ever lived together.

When the time comes to retire, my mother finally makes an honest woman out of herself. She moves to New York for real.

I am, by then, living in Los Angeles. Summoned back east for her retirement festivities as well as assistance moving her into her apartment, a junior one-bedroom in an Upper West Side brownstone more fit for a twenty-five-year-old junior marketing executive than a sixty-three-year-old with arthritic knees, I experience a moment that makes me catch my breath in wrenching self-recognition. On the corner of Columbus Avenue and Seventy-eighth Street, in the rank, piteous humidity of a June evening, stands my mother, father, and brother as well as my mother's brother and his longtime girlfriend, who, fresh off recent travels to Bali or Singapore or God knows where, have come up from Miami. A moving van will come later, but we've spent the afternoon unloading a couple of car trips' worth of items my mother for some reason hadn't wanted to put on the moving truck—pieces of art, pieces of pottery, wicker baskets stuffed with blankets and dishes—into the second-floor walk-up apartment and are en route to dinner.

"Is that the Museum of Natural History?" my uncle inquires. "Well, I'll be."

To which my mother tosses her head to the side and says, well, yes, and there's plenty more great stuff where that came from. Like "really good" restaurants and "a bar I love" and "excellent theater" and "really great stores." She already knows it well, she explains to my uncle and his girlfriend, both of whom are wearing pastel shirts and white pants and neither of whom is sweating as much as my parents and my brother and me; we're all dressed at least partly in black.

She'd been coming into the city for years, my mother continues. This is "really a natural progression." She is "really quite at home" on these streets. "That way is south," she says, pointing to the traffic flow on Columbus Avenue. "Central Park West is the next one over, and it goes north and south."

She knows it. She knows it well. And, of course, not at all. But she knows that, too. As with my father's long-ago cries of "I was just there!" when the Chrysler Building flashed across the television screen during an American Express commercial, her ambition is on a collision course with her innocence, and no one or nothing is to blame except the legacy of striving and all its ruthless discontents. I am by now thirty-five years old, and I know this routine. I am looking at my mother, but I might as well be flipping through snapshots of my own most vulnerable moments: there I am pretending to know my way around school, even though I'm the new kid and can barely find the door; there I am in high school pretending to be friends with people I barely know; there I am in college pretending not to be miserable; there I am as an adult pretending that I don't feel like a child. And as we stand on that corner waiting for the crosswalk light to change, I can see my mother bending over so far backward in an effort to erase the vestiges of her past that I'm afraid her spine will crack right then and there. I want to hug her as much as I want to hit her. But the signal changes, and we proceed forward.

TWO

I'm not proud of this, but I'll come out and say it now. I chose my college not because of its outstanding faculty or its resplendent campus, not because of its fancy-pants reputation or its arty sensibility or its distinguished alumni. I chose my college not so much for what it could offer me while I was there as for what I believed it could deliver me into when I was done: a shabby yet elegant prewar apartment in Manhattan. I wasn't quite sure how I would pay for said apartment—indeed, I had no idea how much such a thing cost—but I was determined to spend the better part of my twenties (and possibly my thirties, forties, fifties, sixties, and seventies) surrounded by houseplants in a sun-drenched if slightly musty one- or two-bedroom overlooking Riverside Drive or West End Avenue. In this apartment, I would drink a lot of coffee while staring out the window. I would read great books and have great lovers, and eventually I'd win a Pulitzer Prize or maybe even a MacArthur "genius" grant for things I'd written while staring out that window. I'd have really great clothes and furniture—all vintage.

For the first seventeen years of my life, thoughts like this didn't cross my mind. As a child and a young teenager I was less concerned with geography than with architecture. Not that I was "concerned" with "architecture" in any significant way (save a passing enthusiasm for *The Fountainhead*). But to the extent that I shared with my mother a fairly nonstop interest in moving to another house, I cared far more about the floor plan than the location. It's true that I was consumed with *Little House on the Prairie* and, by extension, the idea of living "in the country." But I was more interested in the scene inside the house and barn (hence my affection for patchwork quilts and milking stools) than in what surrounded it. When my mother brought me along to open houses, I cared more about what my room would be like than what town or state this house happened to be in.

But when I was seventeen, all that changed in a nanosecond. One evening during the summer before my senior year of high school, my father allowed me to practice my stick-shift skills by driving the Plymouth Horizon into the city. He needed to drop off a score at the apartment of a music copyist who lived on West End Avenue on the Upper West Side. Within moments of my walking into this apartment, a hundred goals and priorities I'd never known I had sprung to life inside me. By the time I'd stepped all the way into the living room, I'd decided that I would simply die if I could not, immediately upon graduating from college, live in such a place.

It was a classic of its genre—a prewar apartment with high ceilings and chipping paint on the window sashes and worn hardwood floors covered by a worn Persian rug. I wasn't privy to the bathroom, but I have no doubt it was a solid, epochal affair with a pedestal sink and original porcelain hexagonal tiles, a few of which were probably cracked around the perimeter. It was modest, far smaller than our house on Jones

Lane, and not the kind of place you'd think would necessarily rock the world of a seventeen-year-old girl. But my world was rocked. Just as my parents, decades earlier, had glimpsed their existential salvation in the pages of *The New Yorker,* I'd seen my future, and it was on West End Avenue. After five minutes in the apartment, I drove home with my father and mounted a strenuous, long-term initiative to point my compass in the direction of that future. I used the preferred method of Ridgewood teenagers: college applications. Due to my abysmal math grades (I'd spent two summers taking remedial algebra), I focused on schools for which I didn't technically have the grades but that might take me because I seemed interesting and creative. In other words, I wasn't going to Yale or Princeton. Though I now suspect I might have had a chance at getting in as some kind of eccentric case—as an "interesting, unconventional candidate"—I wasn't going to Brown either. My high-school guidance counselor, for reasons that mystified me and rankled my mother, wanted me to go to a huge university I'd never heard of in Ohio. Clearly he knew nothing of my real estate plans.

Why I thought that landing in a prewar Manhattan apartment was best accomplished by going to Vassar, a college seventy-five miles north of New York City in the Hudson riverbank city of Poughkeepsie, I don't exactly know. In addition to being swayed by the fact that Meryl Streep had gone there, I recall that I did apply some perverse logic to the decision, most of it based on reading the wedding announcements in *The New York Times* and seeing where various people went to college and imagining, based on their jobs and even their photographs, what kinds of apartments they might live in. I also recall that the longing I felt for such an apartment seemed at the time a direct reaction to life in the suburbs, which I experienced as fundamentally counterfeit and misrepresentative of my true self. I remember feeling (albeit in a vague, unarticulated way) that if I could just have a phone number with a 212 area code—a number, unlike my parents' business line, that connected to an actual phone—I would be able to slough off the residue of my family's disappointments and disenchantments and be my own person in the world. Unlike them, I would be unencumbered and unembarrassed. I would know how to take the subway and, therefore, how to be human.

But these feelings, as turgid as they sound now (which belies how "real" they seemed at the time), weren't the whole story. What I didn't know back then—and, indeed, what I didn't know until after I'd left New York many years later—was that it wasn't the prewar apartment I craved but, rather, an ineffable state of being I can only describe as domestic integrity. This integrity has something to do with being able to not feel like an impostor in your home and, therefore, in your life. For a host of reasons I perceived this as something almost totally absent from our life in Ridgewood. That's not to say (though it's taken me a long time to get to this admission) that it's not available in Ridgewood or any other suburban town, nor am I suggesting that it's a built-in feature of Manhattan apartments. But whereas I long believed that the driving force of my early adulthood was my visceral, sometimes delirious desire to live in New York City, I now realize that my real needs were at once simpler and infinitely more complicated than that. I think I could have walked into any number of domiciles when I was seventeen—a clapboard house in Iowa, a Victorian apartment in Baltimore, a cabin in the woods somewhere—and been knocked over by the same fumes.

But, of course, I didn't and I wasn't. I was focused on New

York. And while I was at Vassar preparing for my life in New York (like my parents before me, preparation was key, which is why I hadn't cut to the chase and gone to New York University or, if I'd had the grades, Columbia), I managed not only to major in English but also to minor in moving.

After my freshman year, I switched residence halls every single semester. With each of these moves, I thought the "integrity" I'd discovered in the music copyist's apartment could be found in the next dorm room, the next cluster of flannel-shirted students watching TV in the parlor, the next impromptu pizza party in the hallway. At the very least, I thought that moving was saving me from some kind of unidentifiable but palpable malaise. In every case, I turned out to be wrong; the next place was always as dissatisfying as the last.

At least I made it through the first year without moving. Occupying one of the smallest doubles in the dorm, a room whose tininess was supposedly mitigated by its having been— of all people—Meryl Streep's (at least according to the residence advisors; I later suspected that this claim was made about any room that was otherwise undesirable), I managed to soldier on. I had a roommate, a genuine WASP with her own beat-up Subaru and a boarding school education who was extraordinarily bright and possessed of a personality that could be by turns captivating and totally maddening. We were fast friends in the beginning until, in a way that seemed both painfully gradual and breathtakingly abrupt, we weren't. Though I'm pretty sure she was as much at sea with herself as I was with myself, our discontent manifested itself on opposite ends of the crazy-girl spectrum. While she was ranting to her dinner companions about gynecological injustices to third-world women, I was holding court with the blank wall over my desk, where I smoked cigarettes and listened to gloomy

Suzanne Vega songs. Undeterred by the cliché of it all, I read poetry, scribbled anguished musings in my notebooks, and spent untold hours wondering if the people around me who appeared to be having so much fun were actually having fun or merely doing imitations of the kinds of people who have fun. When I wasn't pondering such questions, I was occasionally sleeping with a boy who had no intention of being my boyfriend. It was a charmed existence.

Returning to Vassar for my sophomore year (the summer had been a haze of low-paying odd jobs in Ridgewood, including stage-managing one of my mother's summer-stock productions at the high school), I was assigned a large garretlike single on the fifth floor—the top floor, the attic essentially—of the dormitory I'd occupied the previous year. Initially determined to make the best of the situation, I kept the windows permanently ajar to encourage a breeze and decorated the walls with black-and-white art-movie posters—notably an enormous banner for the 1984 cult-hipster film *Stranger Than Paradise*. I also had a luxurious new sleeping implement. Before returning to school, I'd decided that the iron-framed twin beds provided by the college "hurt my back" and thus convinced my parents to buy me a full-sized, canvas-covered futon mattress (all the cool Vassar students had these, though not due to back pain). Once deposited on the floor of my room, as if to signal some combination of earthiness and sexual readiness, I completed the boudoir tableau with a cheap Guatemalan blanket and a candle that had partially melted into an empty beer bottle.

Within days, I was miserable. Though friends initially came over to say hello and check out the room—oh, the grand start-of-semester college tradition of surveying friends' rooms; it is here that the first seeds of house envy begin to sprout—it

wasn't a place anyone would simply swing by on his or her way
to the bathroom or someone else's room, so I had no sponta-
neous visitors. There were a smattering of other rooms on the
floor, but other than a suite of freshman women, the residents
of which were even more morose than I (they preferred the
term "freshpeople"), there rarely appeared to be anyone home.
Meanwhile, the boy with whom I'd occasionally been sleeping
decided he preferred to more-than-occasionally sleep with
someone who would also be known as his girlfriend. I attrib-
uted his interest in her to the fact that her dorm room could be
accessed via just one flight of stairs.

Of course, I knew there were other factors at work. I knew
that, for reasons seemingly beyond my control, I had slipped
into a persona that was fundamentally lame. At least it felt that
way. But this was par for the course. If a student learns nothing else at a liberal arts college, especially one as rife with
gifted, glamorous students as Vassar, he is at least guaranteed
a lesson in insecurity. At least a temporary form of it. At least
until he turns himself upside down and shakes the pieces of
his old self out of him like crumbs in a Pringles can. At least
until he graduates and realizes no one else understands Der-
rida either, so who cares. No exception to this rule, I had by
my second year at Vassar managed to assemble a list of grievances against myself that rivaled those of a major divorce.
Items ranged from anxieties about holding my own alongside my more cultured, better-read classmates (haven't read
Thomas Mann, haven't been to Europe, didn't know there was
a Francis Bacon the painter as well as Francis Bacon the
English guy from a long time ago) to standard-issue self-
loathing about my hair, body, and wardrobe (do not have luxurious Botticelli-like curls like every other girl here, do not have
thighs the circumference of table legs, cannot figure out how

to shop for and wear vintage clothes without looking like a member of the chorus of *Oliver!*). And while I knew on a logical level that none of these hardships were directly linked to my being housed on the fifth floor of a dormitory, I somehow remained convinced that the first step toward a cure involved not a library copy of *Death in Venice* or a junior-year-abroad application but several cardboard boxes and some large plastic bags.

In other words, returning from the holiday break that January, I dropped my bags in the garret, which was hot and airless and strangely muggy even in the dead of winter, and decided that the only way to not wish I could fall asleep and wake up three years later as a full-fledged adult—or at least a college graduate—lay in residing fewer than five flights away from terra firma. I requested a transfer with the housing office. A few days later, I was offered a tiny room on the second floor of a large dorm known for its enthusiastic watchers of the parlor television set. The following Saturday afternoon, I moved my clothes, books, desktop computer (unbearably heavy in those days), and other assorted items down the stairs, across the quad, and into my new quarters. I remember being so determined to do the job smoothly and efficiently that I didn't even detach the stereo speakers from the very large tuner/amplifier (a 1960s relic given to me by my father) to which they were connected. This required putting the whole audio system in a giant box, wires tangling themselves around the various components and curling out the sides like vines, and half carrying/half dragging it to its destination. I'm pretty sure there was snow on the ground.

I remember that I had to move the futon mattress, so I must have enlisted other people to help (despite the glum existence I've described, I did have friends who would have done me such turns), but to this day I have no recollection of who else was involved in this move. Likely, I was already embarrassed by what I was doing. As deranged with unwarranted melancholy as I sometimes was, I wasn't so far gone as not to realize that there were better ways to spend your weekend than hanging your clothes in a new closet and waiting for your new life to start. Deep down (or even not so deep down), I knew that switching dorms was a strenuous but ultimately lazy way of trying to unpeel myself from the morose and rather ridiculous person I'd become since arriving at Vassar the year before.

But like those dreams where you try to scream but can't make a sound, I felt almost physically incapable in college of simply studying or reading or even looking at a piece of art or running around a track. Instead, I spent nearly every waking moment planning my next move: What would I do over the summer? What courses would I take next year? (Never mind that I hadn't read the books for my classes this year.) Where would I live (and what would I wear and what kind of haircut would I have) when I was finally graduated from this place and feeling human again? And because each of those scenarios seemed dependent upon some kind of relocation (insanely, even the question of what courses I'd take was followed quickly by questions as to where would be the best place to live when completing the course work), I'd often find myself lying on my futon and surveying my possessions with an eye toward moving them. How heavy is that bookcase? I'd wonder while lying in bed at 4:00 p.m. How many drawers' worth of clothes could I stuff into one garbage bag? Could I carry three bags at once? Four? Could I carry my printer in one arm and an entire stack of bedding in the other? Could I do this at night so no one would notice?

These weren't just little mind games. Over my remaining

two years at Vassar, I would move seven more times. Please know how much this admission makes me cringe. Counting the moves up just now, I died a little death, not only at the thought of how many books I could have read or chemistry labs I could have taken (though considering I barely got through high-school chemistry, who are we kidding?), but also at the sheer amount of money and time I wasted doing everything in my power to avoid being a regular college kid who did regular college things.

The summer after my sophomore year, instead of working as a camp counselor or getting a Eurorail pass, I insisted on living in Manhattan, where I'd been hired as an intern (at $200 a week, which thrilled me) at an office at Lincoln Center. Having finally acquiesced to my pleas to not spend another summer in Ridgewood, my parents allowed me to sublet the Upper West Side studio of a woman my father knew through work colleagues. The apartment had exposed brick walls and a sleeping loft and, as it happened, was a fifth-floor walk-up in a brownstone (curiously, this fifth-floor situation had none of the unpleasant side effects of the fifth-floor dorm room). The woman who occupied it most of the time was a former actress who was now pursuing a career writing children's musicals about the rodeo circuit. She charged me $800 a month, and I worked out an arrangement with my parents wherein I paid half and they paid half. Astonishingly, I managed to be frugal enough to hold up my end on my $200-a-week income.

It was a hot, hungry, lonely, glorious summer. I was twenty years old, and my life felt like a vast ocean before me. I loved having a real job and living in the city. Though there was no air-conditioning and I had cheap, unflattering work clothes and was so strapped for cash that when I spilled my dinner on the floor one night, I went to bed famished because there was nothing else in the cupboards and I literally couldn't afford to go out and buy a sandwich, I found myself in a state of unparalleled happiness. I loved the buzz of the office, loved the table and chairs on the tar rooftop of the brownstone, and loved the smell of ammonia on the sidewalks outside the Korean grocery markets in the morning.

I loved the people at work so much I wanted to round them up and yoke them to my shoulders as I plowed my way into adulthood. Though I would later realize that most of them were fairly ordinary New Yorkers trying to live decently on the middling salaries of the nonprofit world, I saw them at the time as wildly sophisticated. From my desk in the office, where I typed address labels and stuffed envelopes with a glee I'd never known before, I observed their behavior and listened to them talk on the phone. As far as I was concerned, I was researching the role of my future self. I had crushes on all of them: the men and the women, the old and the young, the glamorous, high-rolling executives and the Brylcreemed accountant. At night, as I drifted off in the airless berth of the sleeping loft, the echoes of their voices in my head were as soothing as the sirens outside.

When my sublet ended in mid-August, I moved back to Ridgewood for a few weeks and completed my internship by commuting to the Port Authority on the Short Line bus. When that was over, I packed up and returned to Vassar. The underwhelm was palpable. The school, which had long ago started to feel like some kind of amusement park for overgrown adolescents, now seemed to have shrunk into an architectural model of itself. It was hard to say what felt more oppressive, the self-congratulatory pride the place took in its ability to offer both limitless freedom and near-foolproof safety or the fact it attracted so much wealth that one student had an original Warhol on the wall of his dorm room.

Despite my new level of exasperation with Vassar, I had a good semester, the best of my whole college experience by far. I lived with three friends in a unit of modern-looking campus apartments designated for upperclassmen. Normally, this housing, which had an open, multilevel design I've always associated with late-1970s-era condos in which groovy singles with feather earrings would play Christopher Cross albums, was reserved for seniors. I, however, had been allowed to enter the housing lottery with three senior friends, and to our delight we'd been granted an apartment. In a statement of opposition against the cult of covering the walls with tapestries and/or huge posters depicting high-contrast black-and-white art photographs, we refused to decorate at all. We were righteous minimalists.

Soon, however, I found myself caught inside yet another escape fantasy.

I did not want to be a college student anymore; I wanted to be a working person living in New York. Now that I had tasted independence, now that I'd known the exultation of turning a key in the solid, wheezing front door of a brownstone, now that I'd known life under the vast canopy of the city, the smallness of the college bordered on the intolerable. In desperation (though perhaps in a stroke of genius?) I applied for and received a one-semester transfer to NYU. I called my beloved colleagues from the Lincoln Center office and talked them into hiring me as a part-time office assistant. I found a $700-a-month one-room apartment in a mildew-scented building in Greenwich Village (another fifth-floor walk-up, as it happened). I then—and this still astounds me—crunched the numbers in such a way that I was able to convince my parents that this scenario wouldn't cost them a dollar more than if I were to finish out the year at Vassar. As I had the previous summer, I'd be paying half my rent—this time $350 per month, which I would easily earn at the Lincoln Center job.

Too distracted by the coming storm of their marital dissolution to put up a fight, my parents granted me permission. And so at Christmas break my father drove the Plymouth Horizon up to Vassar and helped me take the futon mattress and the stereo components (still connected) as well as my computer and books and clothes and a high-contrast black-and-white art photo or two back to Jones Lane. A week later, I loaded it all back into the Horizon and enlisted my father to drive me into the city. I'm pretty sure he did so with reasonable graciousness, which in retrospect seems too kind given the manic, almost embattled attitude I'd developed about my need to get away from both my family and my college. Once installed in my new digs, I stocked the kitchen with ramen noodles and spread out the Guatemalan blanket. I put the Suzanne Vega CDs on the shelf and plugged in the computer. And although I felt like an impostor of staggering proportions, I also couldn't help marveling at myself just a little bit. There I was: a twenty-year-old with her own job and Manhattan apartment. Smoking cigarettes and staring at the wall had taken on entirely new dimensions.

The sped-up version of the subsequent year and a half goes something like this: I lived in the one-room apartment, worked at the nonprofit arts organization, and took NYU classes in dramatic writing (apparently, I was now a playwright). The following summer was the summer that my mother moved out of the house on Jones Lane, and as my parents were no longer able to supply me with $350 in monthly rent money, I was forced to return to Ridgewood and, yet again, commute to Lincoln Center on the bus (it was around this time that I visited my mother's new house and ate polenta with her). In the fall, I returned to Vassar, where I lived in a spacious senior dorm room until I decided I could no longer tolerate eating in the dining hall. At the end of the first semester I rented an off-campus apartment—the second floor of a shabby row house several blocks from campus—with my friend Claire, a premed student whose reasons for living off campus I can no longer remember.

Not that I was planning to live there full-time. By that point, I had amassed almost enough credits to graduate; all I needed to do was write my thesis and attend its accompanying weekly seminar. I no longer wanted to be a playwright, but, rather, a journalist, so I applied for and was granted a three-day-a-week internship at an art magazine in Manhattan. The idea was that I would crash in the apartments of various friends who had already graduated from Vassar or (in a pinch) stay in Ridgewood for the part of the week in which I was doing the internship. I would then return to Vassar once a week for my thesis seminar. Since the campus was only a two-hour train ride from Grand Central Station, this scenario was not implausible, though not exactly advisable either.

I implemented this plan for four days until, on the fifth day, the art magazine went out of business and the entire staff was laid off. Having cleared my calendar of nearly all campus-related activities, I finished out my college career sprawled in front of the television in the row house apartment watching *Little House on the Prairie* reruns and, eventually, news coverage of the 1992 L.A. riots. By graduation day, I had ten addresses under my belt and had moved the futon mattress up and down a total of twelve flights of stairs. My parents drove up and watched me collect my diploma. They told me they were proud. This made me incredibly guilty and, by extension, incredibly sad.

But guess what was coming my way? A slightly shabby prewar apartment on 100th Street between West End Avenue and Riverside Drive. I had a friend named Lara, whom I'd met at the Lincoln Center office, and together we'd decided to look for a place somewhere on the West Side, between Ninety-sixth Street and the Columbia University campus. Though she'd been living downtown, she was set to enroll in film school at Columbia, and though I'd be working in midtown— I'd reluctantly accepted a job as an editorial assistant at a beauty magazine—I still wanted to live among the Gothic spires and bearded socialists of the upper stretches of West End Avenue. So during the first month or so of that job, while I commuted in from Ridgewood on the dreaded Short Line bus, Lara scoured the apartment listings until she happened upon the place on West 100th Street. And when we looked at it and were told we didn't have enough income to qualify, Lara visited the management office, security deposit and first month's rent in hand, every day for three weeks until the land-lord finally broke down and rented it to us. Preposterously, we both had to get our parents to sign guarantors' letters stating (falsely) that their yearly incomes were a hundred times the monthly rent. I have known very few young people who've managed to get leases in New York City without producing this kind of document, which all landlords know is bogus but seems to comfort them nonetheless. The rent (this figure is permanently etched in my mind) was $1,776.76. Since we still couldn't afford the place without a third roommate, I called a

Vassar friend, Ben, and offered him in on the deal. He immediately agreed.

As far as I was concerned, this apartment was paradise. Not
to mention huge. A long hallway ran the length of the place,
off of which lay a decent-sized living room, a dining room, and
a large bedroom. At the end of the hall was a tiny bedroom,
and adjacent to that was the bathroom and kitchen, both of
which I also considered ample and therefore evidence of my
ascending station in life. My room was the dining room, which
had been converted into a separate bedroom. Lara, being envi-
ably assertive (she is now a movie director), had the large bedroom, and Ben, being gracious and patient to a fault (he was
then a third-grade teacher), took the small room. The whole
apartment was probably about eleven hundred square feet. My
share was $550.

Oh, and the bathroom, whose sole window afforded privacy
by way of a faded and paint-splattered stained-glass panel in a
Victorian fleur-de-lis pattern, had the original porcelain hexagonal tiles. Clearly I was where I was meant to be.

With the exception of my job, which reverberated with so
much displaced female anger that I often broke out in hives, I
adored my life here. I adored Ben and Lara and I adored the
apartment and I adored just about everything we did in it: the
meals we ate, the episodes of *Northern Exposure* that Ben and
I watched, the parties we threw in which strangers crowded
in the kitchen and lit their cigarettes off the stove. I had a
boyfriend—a twenty-nine-year-old journalist who seemed
extremely grown up—and even though he had his own apartment downtown with a doorman and air-conditioning, I often
wanted nothing more than to be sprawled out on the couch in
the apartment on 100th Street with my age-appropriate peers

doing age-appropriate things like eating lentils from the 99-cent store.

The building, which wasn't in any way fancy but had a handsome marble lobby and ornate ironwork on the front door, was, as far as I was concerned, one of the most beautiful things I'd ever seen. It smelled like a combination of that musty, uriney smell that imbues all New York City buildings and the chicken and plantains that were frequently cooking in the ground-floor apartment of the Puerto Rican superintendent, Carlos, and his enormous extended family. One member of this family, a woman of indeterminate age named Carmen, had a habit of using the super's keys to enter apartments when tenants weren't home. She wouldn't steal anything but, rather, identify certain items that appeared to be broken or not in use and later ask if she could have them. I remember her approaching me while I was retrieving the mail and informing me that my Walkman, which I kept in a desk drawer, didn't rewind properly but that she'd take it off my hands for five bucks.

The neighborhood was hardly unsafe. But back in 1992, if you worked at a magazine for which the question of how best to apply lip liner required regular summit meetings, it was considered a bit unusual to live north of Ninety-sixth Street. Many of my co-workers were comely trust funders with co-op studios on lower Fifth Avenue and time-shares in the Hamptons, and I remember taking a smug delight in their bewildered, slightly appalled reactions to my address. "One Hundredth Street?" they'd ask. "Isn't that Harlem?"

Eventually, Ben and Lara moved out and got their own places. I stayed for five years (mind-blowing considering my college record) and rotated through five more roommates, a few of whom became friends for life and a few of whom I can barely remember. One roommate incident that I do remember but wish I could erase from my mind involved a certain Columbia grad student I'll call Brad.

I cannot overemphasize the degree to which this apartment was a highly desirable "share" situation. Given that the building was rent stabilized, the unit was at least 20 percent cheaper than most Manhattan apartments—and significantly larger and nicer to boot. Whenever a roommate moved out, the only action necessary to replace him or her was to post a Room Available sign on a handful of telephone poles on Broadway. Within an hour, at least a dozen people would have called and begged to come over "right away" before someone else snapped it up.

Partly because we were busy and partly because having a coveted apartment tends to strip its occupants of all traces of empathy, it became a tradition that roommate candidates would be interviewed on a single day, one after the other. We'd show them the place, make them explain themselves, and then tell them we'd call them if we were interested. Brad was among a group of candidates being considered to replace Pat, a particularly beloved roommate who'd been attempting to write her doctoral dissertation in the tiny room once occupied by Ben. The remaining roommate was Stephanie, a struggling actress I also adored and with whom I'd be deciding who should be crowned Our Next Roommate. On the day we interviewed Brad, we'd also interviewed several other nice people. One was a woman who was a Ph.D. candidate at Columbia but spent most of her time in Russia. Pat, who'd overheard some of the interviews as she was packing up her room (and who was also more than a decade older and much, much wiser), suggested to us that the Russian scholar was the way to go, since it would be like hardly having a third roommate at all.

Brad, she'd pointed out to us, seemed immature and puppy dog–like and, did we happen to notice, mentioned his mother no fewer than twelve times.

Being twenty-five and all, we chose Brad anyway. The reason we did this is that we wanted boyfriends (I was long done with the twenty-nine-year-old journalist; Stephanie was doing too much musical theater for her own good). Not that we wanted *him* as a boyfriend. But Brad had the distinct advantage of being a boy. And since he'd be attending graduate school at Columbia in the fall, it was likely he'd be bringing friends to the apartment. Possibly those friends would be cute and smart and the kinds of people we might date. Never mind Pat's point that Brad was in the English department, where there were considerably more women than men. Never mind that by then I, too, was in a graduate program at Columbia and should have known that if you wanted a boyfriend, the chances of finding one in a humanities department were only slightly better than the chances of finding one in a handbag store. At that point in my life, hard evidence was less compelling than sweet, soft fantasy. I took Brad's deposit check and handed him a set of keys.

Brad's first offense was to bring in a large piece of baby blue carpeting and unroll it in his room so that it covered every inch of floor. He then moved in a shiny brown Formica desk of the sort you see in bank branches. Then an enormous bright orange recliner.

I need to say a few things about the decor and overall architectural style of this apartment. By no means was it luxuriously or even interestingly furnished. Just about everything was a hand-me-down from someone's parents' house or some kind of "gem" (when you're in your early twenties "gem" is a broad category) dragged in from off the street. We had a large, comfortable sofa whose appearance I no longer recall but that I have no doubt was reasonably attractive or at least minimalist and nonoffensive. The walls were lined with bookshelves, over which Calder prints and collector's edition posters from events sponsored by the Lincoln Center office hung in stark black frames. In the kitchen we had a sea green 1950s-era breakfast table and two matching adorable if somewhat rickety chairs (there had been three until Ben sat down in one and it splintered into pieces right out from under him). Our bedrooms were generally spare and book filled. Worn, faded Oriental rugs seemed to slide in and out as roommates moved in and departed. Houseplants would thrive for a few weeks, then singe to their deaths in the sunlight from the south-facing windows, the desiccated leaves falling behind the couch never to be swept up. We occasionally vacuumed and dusted, but we never waxed the floors. Dried flowers in random-sized clay pots popped up in unlikely corners. When we played music, it was often jazz or the work of esoteric South American folk musicians. When people came over for the first time, they said, "*Amazing* place." You get the picture.

Brad, for his part, did not get the picture. In the first weeks, he holed up in his carpeted room, listening to U2 and reading his Melville and his Hawthorne and occasionally wondering aloud to Stephanie and me why he wasn't quite "clicking" with anyone in the English Department. In the weeks after that, he became so aggrieved at the conditions of the cupboards in which he'd been forced to store his mother's expensive cookware that he embarked on a cleaning frenzy whose results defied everything he thought he knew about the physical laws of hygiene.

Unlike the disinfected Westchester County house in which Brad had grown up, the apartment on 100th Street was one of those unrenovated prewar New York City dwellings for which total cleanliness was simply impossible. No matter how hard you scrubbed and how many cleaning products you used, there would always be a layer of grime on the counters, on the windowsills, and in crevices of the woodwork. No matter how many roach traps you set down, there would always be that momentary flurry of activity when you turned the lights on in the middle of the night. No matter how pristine the contact paper on the bottoms of the drawers or the shelves of the cabinets, there was never any guarantee that at some moment in the recent or distant past, a mouse hadn't padded across someone's mom's Le Creuset frying pan like a mischievous cartoon character. For Brad, there must have been something almost primitive about the place. Appalled by our sanitation standards, confused by our decor tastes, and, as time went on, so tongue-tied around us that he resorted to making embarrassing puns or recounting his college days in excruciating—and mind-numbing—detail, Brad grew both more irritated and more irritating by the day.

I, in turn, grew despairing. This was an intruder. There was no other way to put it. For the first time in the three years I'd lived in the apartment, I felt as if I'd lost control of it. And since the place almost literally reverberated with the echoes of my own self-approval—the slam of the lobby doors, the lurching and cranking of the elevator, the tinny rattle of the mailboxes; this was the sound track of my life as the person I'd always wanted to be—I couldn't keep myself from feeling that something precious had been snatched away. Whereas once the apartment had been a cozy backdrop for an ever-evolving production of *Three's Company* as reimagined by Woody Allen, it now seemed as impersonal and juvenile as a college dormitory. Whereas once I'd actually looked forward to the sound of my roommates' keys in the door, I now held my breath when I heard footsteps in the hallway. Whereas once I'd been convinced that the threesome dynamic offered the best chances for roommate mental health and harmony (if one person didn't feel like making macaroni and cheese and whining about entry-level jobs, someone else almost certainly did), I could now feel the balance shifting toward something that looked like war.

And then came the first shot. One evening, as I was writing in my room, Brad knocked on the door (doors were always closed now) and asked if he could borrow my suede jacket.

This jacket, a slightly too large 1970s brown car coat with a torn satin lining and wide lapels, had quite possibly been my greatest source of happiness in college and was now my second-greatest source of happiness (the first, of course, being the apartment in its pre-Brad incarnation). Brad had complimented it many times before and even asked once to try it on (it fit him, if snugly) but had never asked to wear it. Faced with this sudden boldness, I was too stunned to know what to say. Finally, I asked how long he planned on wearing it, and he said it would just be for the night. Still dumbfounded, I said okay (I could not at that moment find the words to say anything else), and he took the jacket from my bed, put it on, and left the house.

What happened next—or, I should say, what happened soon after this—still horrifies me a bit. When I allow myself to shuffle through my life's most guilt-producing memories, this one invariably rises to the top of the pile. What happened was that I became absolutely convinced that Brad had to leave the apartment. Though I knew perfectly well that the reason he was there was because I had made the selfish, myopic mistake of inviting him, though I also knew that he'd borrowed my

jacket because he was as lonely and desperate for social connections as anyone I'd ever known, I also knew that if he
remained in my space for another week, I might choke on the
bile of my own pitiable mistake.

Still, weeks passed and I did nothing, which is to say I did
nothing but complain about Brad to anyone who would listen.
I knew kicking him out was unconscionable, but I also
believed that every day I continued to live with him was a day
so miserable I might as well have spent it in an iron lung.
Pretty soon, the dilemma became the central problem of my
life. It consumed me. As though I were sending copies of the
same letter to multiple advice columnists, I laid the scenario
out to my friends, my co-workers at my various temp jobs, and,
of course, Stephanie, who was similarly annoyed (if not totally
vexed) by the situation. I even considered actually writing a
letter to an advice columnist but, knowing the likely response,
did not. Meanwhile, the advice I received felt lukewarm. People who were more compassionate and even tempered than I
told me to suck it up and cope with him at least until the end
of the school year. People who'd known me for longer pointed
out that I already knew what I was going to do so why not just
get it done. My mother told me it was unfair to throw him out
for no reason but that the baby blue carpet really did sound
awful. My friend Alison, a Columbia classmate who was by
now my best friend, labeled my Brad-related strategy sessions
"bradegizing." Finally she suggested I simply lay his carpet out
on the sidewalk along with his bed and his reclining chair and
hope he wouldn't notice that his room had been relocated.

In lieu of that option, I summoned Stephanie. I told her we
had to ask Brad to leave. I told her that our lives were passing
us by, that we wouldn't be young and carefree and living in
this apartment forever, that it was criminal to waste our salad

days, not to mention our wonderful, majestic, perfect-in-a-way-Brad-was-incapable-of-appreciating apartment on someone who covered the oak parquet floors with baby blue carpet. Stephanie was hesitant, but she acquiesced. (I'd like to think this was because his presence was as intolerable to her as it was to me, but in truth it was probably because I was the "senior roommate" and she felt pressured.)

That evening, we knocked on Brad's door and asked to speak with him. He was, as usual, listening to U2 and staring numbly at his computer screen. I remember that I was shaking with anxiety and that I felt like an unforgivable asshole even though I hadn't said anything yet. I remember that my jacket, which had been promptly and safely returned by Brad after his night out with it, was hanging on the back of my desk chair in my room, no worse for the wear. I remember knowing at the time that none of what I was about to say had anything to do with the jacket, but that I was planning on leading with that subject anyway.

There's very little else that I remember.

There was a look of shock and anger, some stammering, and some silence. Stephanie and I finished the deed (did she say anything during the exchange? I honestly can't recall) and retreated to my room with the door closed, hearts beating as though we'd just averted a mugger on the sidewalk. After a few minutes, we heard Brad storm down the hallway, open the front door, and slam it with a force whose sound I can still conjure today. The framed Calder prints rattled on the walls. The *New Yorker* magazines fluttered momentarily in the gust. Stephanie and I probably said something to each other like "At least it's done." Or maybe she said nothing and I wrung my hands and made murmurings about how I'd had no choice, that I knew that asking him to leave on the grounds of simply not liking him was really, really, really terrible but I just couldn't go on otherwise.

In any case, it was both done and not done. Brad did not speak to us anymore, but nor did he move out. Like a breakup that can never make the leap from imminence to actuality, Brad's time on West 100th Street stretched into another tortured two months. When he failed to pay his rent, I knocked on his door once again and asked if he was planning to use his security deposit in lieu of a check. He shrugged and mumbled something that sounded like yes. When another month passed and he had neither moved nor paid his rent again, I told him he had a week to get out. I honestly can't remember what happened after that. I have no memory of him rolling up his carpet or moving his furniture, nor do I recall getting his keys back or saying goodbye. I do remember that the pickings were rather slim on the next round of roommate selections and that the woman we chose to replace him, a twenty-two-year-old aspiring advertising executive with a baby voice and a penchant for rubbing her toes with nail polish remover while smoking Merit Ultra Lights, was almost as disturbing a presence as Brad was, albeit in a totally different way.

While I try to piece together the order of events surrounding Brad, what's most striking is the amount of amnesia that set in even within weeks of the initial confrontation. In the fourteen years that have elapsed since this took place, I have not until writing this book forced myself to recount the details of what I did. I've casually said to people, "I kicked out a roommate once," but I suspect that even as I've said it, the words had already twisted themselves around a false mythology. Surely, I'd kicked out my roommate because he was crazy or abusing drugs or not paying his rent. Surely, some sacrosanct line had been crossed, and I'd kicked him out because that's what a reasonable person does in that situation. Since I am a generally good-natured and fair-minded person, it couldn't possibly have been any other way. Could it?

If this had not been a matter of real estate, if my relationship to Brad had been circumscribed within the context of work or casual friends or some kind of extracurricular activity, it's almost certain that when faced with the sudden desire never to see him again, I would have acted judiciously, or at least agonized about it for far longer than a few months. But just as my various college residences had engendered in me a sickness whose only cure was to move out as quickly as possible, the presence of Brad in the West 100th Street apartment seemed more like a form of psychological torture than the simple bummer that it actually was and should have felt like. And because that apartment was the first place I'd lived in either my childhood or my adult life that not only felt like home but also embodied everything I'd ever fantasized about a home, I was willing to sacrifice not only my manners but even a little bit of my humanity in order to protect it. As a result, I did to Brad what I refused to do even to the cockroaches in the corners. I stepped on him and then erased him from my mind.

That story is shameful, but it's also, in its own sad way, a field guide for the perverse machinations of my lifelong housing neuroses. As though my living quarters were a holy land that faced a constant threat of invasion or defacement, I maintained a relentless—and exhausting—posture of defensiveness. Worse, it was a defensiveness born of irrationality. What, after all, had been the harm in Brad borrowing my jacket? What level of threat, despite its resemblance to something that would cover the floor of a suburban bedroom in 1976 (come to think of it, it probably had), was that blue carpet posing to my well-being? These are simple questions with simple answers—namely, "none" and "none"—but at the time they seemed not only unanswerable but also possibly dangerous by virtue of their very existence. I did not, in other words, feel I could live in an apartment in which those questions arose. Moreover, this was a matter not of my happiness but of my survival. At least that's how I saw it at the time, which is to say I was bonkers.

Ironically, by the time of Brad's departure, much of the magic of the apartment on West 100th Street was wearing off. I was by then twenty-six years old. By New York City standards, this was (and is) a perfectly acceptable age at which to be sharing an apartment (indeed, I knew forty-five-year-olds who were still writing their names on food containers in the refrigerator). And though I still loved the apartment with the kind of desperate, clinging urgency usually reserved for first-time adolescent romance, there's no denying that it wasn't offering as many benefits as it once had. As I grew older and the roommate turnover rate grew higher, the place felt less like a source of emotional and aesthetic ballast than a crash pad I'd mistaken for a permanent residence. Worse, as my cohabitants became younger, my "senior roommate" status began to feel less like a mark of distinction than like a big-city version of being a college student who can't bring himself to graduate even though he's approaching thirty.

In other words, my eye was wandering. As would be my wont for the better part of the next decade, I was having visions—all of them about housing. At any given time, I was mentally buying furniture, being the sole hostess of imaginary dinner parties, doing math equations to figure out how much rent I could afford. And whereas I'd once confined my domestic fantasies to the idea of living in the apartment with *just one* other roommate (a huge indulgence), I began to entertain decadent thoughts of living there alone. And because that was an impossible notion (the place was a hedonistic eleven hundred square feet, and though the rent had gone up only slightly from our original $1,776.76 it was still entirely too high for one person!), I soon became preoccupied with the next-best thing: finding another (smaller, cheaper) apartment.

I should step back and fill in a few more details about what else transpired during my years on West 100th Street. In addition to eating a lot of macaroni and cheese and watching a lot of MTV's *Real World* (the first season, mind you, which seemed at the time like groundbreaking entertainment) and having enough fun to make up for the lack of fun in my college years, I was trying to get some kind of career going, preferably as a writer and preferably as the kind that gets paid for things she writes. And while I wrote very little during that time that doesn't now make me wince with the kind of mortification you actually feel in your bloodstream, I'd be lying if I said that these weren't arguably the most important years of my professional life. So when I look back on my twenties, I think it's fair to say that I didn't devote *all* my energy to unfair treatment of certain roommates. For all my shenanigans—and this would include dating absurdly neurotic and egocentric men as well as spending too much time in bars pontificating about the state of contemporary fiction—I was also working my ass off. I was writing articles for women's magazines—"Life in a Jealousy Minefield," "Finding the Cheerleader Within," "How to Know If You're Grooming Too Much"—and, after rewriting them five times, getting them killed. I was sweating over book proposals—"Feminist Kitsch: How the Women's Movement Was Hijacked by 'Women's Media' and the Cult of Self-Improvement," "Memoirs of a Commercial Girlhood: Growing

Up with a Jingle Writer Dad," "Untitled Book About All the Ways That Generation X Is Screwed by Baby Boomers"—that never made it within ten blocks of a publisher's office. Mostly, though, I was working many, many, *many* secretarial temp jobs—Bear Stearns, Goldman Sachs, the Hanna-Barbera licensing department of Time Warner Entertainment (where I was privy to several highly confidential contracts regarding the usage of the likeness of Fred Flintstone).

But if the road to becoming a professional writer felt like the main artery of my life, my preoccupation with housing functioned as blood itself. Sure, there were periods during which my desire for nice real estate graciously stepped aside to make room for some more pressing desire—like spending meaningful evenings listening to Lou Reed in the dark with some new paramour—but I don't think it's an exaggeration to say that most of my emotional energy and even some inexplicable measure of sexual energy were tied up in thinking about places where I could live. And if you'll pardon the expression, this produced excruciating cases of blue balls. As though lofts in TriBeCa existed solely for the purposes of taunting me from the luxury real estate pages of *The New York Times Magazine,* I sometimes found it difficult to read the Sunday paper without writhing in envy. As though majestic prewar apartment buildings were attractive people at a party who were at once close enough to touch and, for real or imaginary reasons, devastatingly out of reach, I was not capable of walking by certain edifices on Riverside Drive or Central Park West without feeling the ache of rejection.

And that is how I came to be the president of my own personal academy of domestic desire, the overseer of a pantheon of architectural structures and corresponding price tags that led to the most adolescent form of existential inquiry: Where should I live? Why can't I afford to live where I want to live? How come *where* I live is so tied up in *why* I live? More than a decade later, I still haven't answered those questions, but I've packed enough boxes and filled out enough change-of-address forms to know that with real estate, as with romance, the thrill is quite often in the chase. During the last year that I lived on West 100th Street, I spent more weekends than not looking at apartments that I couldn't really afford, wandering through furniture stores whose goods were well beyond my means (there was at least one incident of hyperventilation at ABC Carpet & Home), and desperately trying to think of what I could do to earn enough money to afford at least six hundred square feet of my very own.

This period marked the beginning of what I now think of as phase one of my full-blown real estate obsession: the hypothetical phase. It was hypothetical because my excitement levels around real estate—either the kind you buy or the kind you rent—ran in inverse proportion to my ability to afford it. I was hardly alone in this, of course. I've always said: you haven't lived in New York City until you've thrown up out the window of a taxi or wanted to put a bullet in your head because you're so envious of someone else's square footage (life in a jealousy minefield, indeed). But part of what made the hypothetical phase so wrenching was the way my mind would often become ensnarled in certain concepts having to do with merit. I did not have my fantasy apartment, I rationalized, because I had not yet done anything to deserve it. I hadn't written the book, secured the prestigious magazine contract, or had an article optioned for a movie. And since I was frequently convinced that my professional ambitions were destined to be thwarted no matter how hard I worked or how many book signings I attended in the hopes of meeting some editor who would find me terribly witty and demand to see my prose immediately, the scarcity complex that surrounded my work life soon extended its reach to my feelings about real estate. Afraid I'd never have anything, I lusted after everything.

That's when the dreams began. Almost every night, images of houses and apartments would glide through my head like impish little angels. There were fine penthouses, sun-drenched "classic sixes" on the Upper West Side, and cozy downtown studios with kitchenettes and loft beds. There were cavernous, empty brownstones that echoed with the promise of furnishings to come. There were awful tenements with rats on the counters and junkies in the stairway. In some dreams I was an active participant: I'd be a new occupant who'd lost the key, a would-be renter whose hands would freeze while trying to write a check, a maid for whom the dust wouldn't disappear. In others, the living spaces would just float across my brain like clouds, baiting me with their improbable grandeur or unbearable grimness, leaving me crushed—or relieved—when I awoke to find myself in the same cluttered room in the same crowded apartment in which I'd fallen asleep.

There were also, of course, "extra room" dreams. They're a staple of real estate dreams, and unlike dreams about unknown spaces I have more of them as I get older. In these dreams I'm walking through my home—either my actual home or some random floor plan my subconscious has labeled "home"—and suddenly stumble upon a new room, sometimes even an entirely new wing. Like the feeling one gets upon finding a wad of cash in an old coat pocket, there's both an elation and a pang of guilt in these dreams. No sooner have I marveled at my discovery and pondered all its exhilarating possibilities than I am overcome with shame at my poor observational skills. How could I have lived here all this time and not noticed this room? How dare I have griped about my cramped quarters when all this square footage was right under my nose.

Psychoanalysts and others who have an interest in dream interpretation (such as girlfriends sitting around with you at a wine bar) will tell you that the extra-room dream signifies a desire for new opportunities. I once stumbled upon a Web site called Dream Doctor, which said such a dream is common in women "who have sacrificed personal hobbies and passions like painting, music, desire to own a small business for the responsibility of parenting." I don't really buy that, since in a dozen years of having that dream, I haven't been tempted to make any sacrifices in order to become a parent and, besides, I know plenty of men who've had the extra-room dream, too. But I do wonder sometimes if this dream crops up out of some perverse force of goodwill. It is, after all, a dream about abundance. It's about being able to stretch out, about being surprised by the size of your own footprint. And although once, in my thirties, I awoke from an extra-room dream with an unwavering certainty that my unconscious mind had just commanded me to extricate myself from a relationship that was on a slow crawl toward nowhere (there was, quite literally, too much room between me and the man in question; we were a house so oversized that love could only get lost wandering the hallways), I've generally kept it in my psyche's positive column.

But that's because no number of extra-room dreams or "if only you lived here" or "thank God you don't live there" dreams can pack quite the neurotic punch of a dream I had during that last year on West 100th Street. In this dream, I am informed that a stunningly gorgeous stand-alone house is available for immediate occupancy. The house, which is spacious without being unmanageably large and appears to be the architectural love child of a California Craftsman and a Japanese pagoda, is in the middle of Manhattan and also in the middle of some sort of pastoral wonderland. Trees and grass and flowering bushes surround it. Petals from cherry blossom trees, not exactly a prominent botanical presence in New York City, dapple the driveway and the front steps like snowflakes. No other houses are near it. In fact, no people are near it. The park is encircled by an iron fence, and the gate to that fence is locked. It looks like Gramercy Park, except it's about ten times the size.

The rent is $127 a month.

Who gets this house? Someone "deserving." Someone "accomplished." Someone "extremely successful and interesting." In the dream, as the criteria for occupying this piece of paradise are explained to me (who's doing the explaining? Surely the same mythic beast that kept my parents in southern Illinois too long and later evilly coerced them into moving to Ridgewood because they "weren't ready" for New York), I can feel my blood pressure rising past the Manhattan skyline itself. A gust carrying hundreds of cherry blossoms hurls toward me, and after that the self-doubt rains down like locusts. Am I deserving? Am I interesting? What about "extremely" interesting? Who are these judges, and what can I do to convince them how much I deserve this house? Who is my competition, and what have they achieved that I have not? What can I do to get this one break? How completely and utterly fantastic would my life be if lightning struck and I was given this one extraordinary gift?

Et cetera.

There is nothing more to say, clearly. Indeed, there was nothing even to say back when I had the dream. At that time, I woke up, scribbled its major plot points into a notebook, and stared at the page until all I could do was shake my head and smile. Later that year, upon finding a not perfect but entirely decent rent-stabilized one-bedroom sublet (possibly not entirely legal) on West Eighty-sixth Street, I said goodbye to West 100th Street. This wasn't as sad a parting as I'd feared. I didn't love the new neighborhood, that's for sure (though it was a mere fourteen blocks south of 100th Street, it seemed a whole other world, one involving numerous paint-your-own-ceramics studios). But the apartment, despite its minuscule kitchen and unremarkable bathroom (no stained-glass window, but there were porcelain hexagonal tiles), was a genuine one-bedroom unit in a solid old building with a part-time doorman. The rent was $1,054 a month, an amount I could almost manage. And though I could have stayed on West 100th with one roommate and paid slightly less than $1,054, the novelty of living alone seemed worth the extra expense. For the first time in my life, I even hired real movers.

The movers carried the futon into the new place. For the first time in twelve moves, I did not lay a finger on that futon. I stood there and watched. This was triumphant, a revelation, the beginning of a new regime. And then, of course, that special brand of shittiness known as New York shittiness—"not quite civilized," I could hear my father say—fell into the apartment like a bomb. The building superintendent appeared suddenly in the doorway and began shouting at the movers in Spanish (which, being Israeli, they didn't understand). It was a sharp, furious, ugly shouting—barking, really—and I remember that I was reaching into a high cupboard putting dishes away and was so startled that I nearly knocked a set of glasses off the counter. The super was a man possessed, a man who was apparently out of the loop and apparently deeply distressed about it. "You don't live here!" he roared in broken English. "No one says you can live here! You get out now!"

Out on the street, he'd ordered the movers not to take anything else off the truck. When I explained that I had a longstanding agreement to sublet the apartment, he said he didn't know about it and that therefore it wasn't true. When I offered to call the woman from whom I was subletting and let him talk to her, he said this would accomplish nothing. He said I needed something called "proof of residency." He said he needed to be involved in this transaction, though he wouldn't specify in what way. And after twenty minutes of screaming and crying and hysterical calls to various people who couldn't do anything (Alison, Stephanie, the guy I was dating, the guy I'd dated before this new guy), I started to understand what "proof of residency" meant. It meant baksheesh. It meant cash. Of course. So I went down the street to the ATM and took $100 out of my already overdrawn bank account and returned to the building with my "proof." He accepted it as though it were a complete surprise and then let the movers resume. It would be the first of many fistfuls of proof I would hand over to this man. In fact, in the ensuing two years, the cost of simply staying afloat in the city and having a modicum of fun would break me. And sooner rather than later, I would grow so tired of feeding the city's various angry beasts that I would leave it for good. But that night, I had won. I was twenty-seven, the age my mother had been when I was born. And as I lay on my futon, counting the notches in the ceiling molding, I felt as if I were finally peeking out from underneath the covers of my youth. I was home. At least for a time. And even if I wound up being a failure in a thousand other ways, no one would ever be able to say I hadn't done so on my own.

THREE

For a long time, I believed I was enthralled by the *Little House on the Prairie* idea because it was just that: an idea. It was a narrative, not a viable lifestyle option. I believed the reason I gasped in delight whenever I happened upon an episode on TV was that it transported me to a rural idyll that was intriguing in theory but that I would surely hate in real life. In other words, I was never going there. I was just going to watch. It's odd, then, that in my twenties, despite my devotion to urbanity, I often found myself wrestling with a curiosity about country living that seemed strangely akin to a homophobic person "struggling with same-sex attraction." As much as I wanted to be a creature of the city, as much as I'd organized my entire life around the overpriced, undersized vagaries of Manhattan living, I sometimes found myself wanting desperately to live on a farm, or at least near one. I can't explain this by way of any rational desire; indeed, it was almost purely visceral. I wanted to smell the countryside, to hear it. I wanted to live someplace where the evenings were punctuated by the sound of a wooden screen door slamming shut. And though this longing could be temporarily extinguished by dull weekends in upstate New York among oppressive mosquitoes and anxious friends (with their inevitable freak-outs over how to properly caramelize onions and who's on cleanup duty), the thought of leaving the city and plopping myself down in Laura Ingalls country only got more beguiling as I got older.

The other thing happening as I got older was that my life in the city was beginning to take on the qualities of a pair of shoes you've been wearing forever and now have holes and smell slightly of Camembert but somehow can't bring yourself to throw away. Though I loved my friends, I was tired of the cantankerous, money-extorting building super, tired of hot, airless subway platforms, tired of knowing that no matter how much I earned or how "deserving" I was, I'd probably still never live in the kind of apartment I really wanted. And so, when I was twenty-nine, I tossed out my old shoes. I gave up my sublet, put my few pieces of furniture on a long-distance moving truck, and got on a plane for Lincoln, Nebraska.

I realize that it can be difficult to make sense of this move. Even ten years out—and I am writing this book almost exactly a decade after I boarded that TWA jet and flew from LaGuardia to St. Louis to Lincoln—the whole experience remains something of a delicious enigma. For all its fine qualities, Lincoln is not exactly one of the nation's premier destinations. It has no seaport or famous cuisine. It's unlikely to be written up in an in-flight magazine as "one of the heartland's hidden gems." From certain angles, it can almost look like a caricature of Midwestern banality. There's the requisite "rich" side of town, where the country-club district gives way to swirling cul-de-sacs of McMansions and jumbo-sized Macaroni Grill and Outback Steakhouse restaurants outside of which cherubic families clutch beepers that will vibrate when their tables are ready. There's the "poor" side, where weathered

Victorian houses have been converted into low-rent apartment buildings, where coffee canisters filled with cigarette butts sit on porches like statuary, where immigrants from Mexico and Vietnam and Iraq work multiple minimum-wage jobs and commingle—somewhat uneasily—with white folks who've been laid off from factories or are living on disability. In between these areas there's the main campus of the University of Nebraska and the capitol building and the Haymarket district with loftlike antiques stores and a vegan sandwich shop and some elegant old neighborhoods with copper pots hanging from racks.

To say that I wasn't swayed by the succor of those latter neighborhoods, to insist I wasn't unconsciously channeling my mother's never fully realized desire to cloak herself in the cozy snobberies—so "classy" yet so affordable—of college town life, would not be entirely honest. Indeed, I remember being shocked that some version of "the life of the mind" and all its attendant Persian rugs and Bach festival posters was apparently available—and for far, far less money—in venues other than Central Park West. But my fascination with Lincoln went beyond its favorable exchange rate with Manhattan. At the risk of sounding mystical or callow or, worse, unaccountable for my choices, I have to say that my decision to move there felt less like a decision than a decree from some otherworldly authority. I didn't just want to do it; I had to do it.

I had to do it because I had somehow managed to live almost three decades without feeling as if I could perform basic adult tasks. Thanks to the infantilizing embrace of Manhattan, I had never owned a car, never (at least as an adult) raked the leaves or shoveled the snow of my own yard, never had the experience of going to a supermarket, buying a large amount of groceries, and, rather than carrying them several blocks home like a bedraggled mule and then shoving them into shallow cupboards, simply loading them into the car and then unloading them into the proper storage space in a proper kitchen. I realize these examples sound quotidian and therefore kind of adolescent—the hallmarks of adulthood as seen by a young girl tugging at her mother's skirt. But I cannot overemphasize the degree to which I felt that certain fundamental life experiences had eluded me in a way that rendered me practically paralyzed. True, by the standards of the city I could get along well enough. I could find my way to temp jobs and to TriBeCa restaurants, and no siren or car alarm or street hollering was too loud to keep me awake at night. But in the outside world, in places (on the rare occasions I visited them) where the vast blankness of the land and sky made even the enormous supermarkets seem tiny, where, to many, words like "Vassar" were just a random sequence of letters, where weather mattered more than most anything else, I often felt lost, irrelevant, fatuous.

I moved to Lincoln because I did not want to continue in this vein. On a more practical level, I also moved there because it was incredibly cheap. Because this reason was—and is—simpler to explain to others, it's the one I still tend to trot out when fielding questions about the whole episode. Courtesy mainly of student loans but also of rent that was "almost manageable" rather than actually manageable, I was now approximately $80,000 in debt. Because of this debt, I told myself—and a lot of other people—that the abrupt turn in my life trajectory had come out of desperation. I told myself that I had "no choice" but to move to Nebraska (as if it were a modern-day debtors' prison) and begin the process of getting unbroke. But this was a lie; even at the time I knew it was a lie. If cleaning up my finances had been my only goal, I could have just found a full-time, high-paying (or at least better-paying) job with benefits and stayed in New York. If my rent was truly my biggest problem, I could have moved to Queens or Hoboken and commuted to this job like a normal, hardworking person. But the truth was that the move wasn't really motivated by money. It was motivated by a fierce and frightening desire. This desire was two-tiered. The first tier was that as much as I sometimes yearned for a full-time, high-paying job with benefits, I wanted more to remain what I already was: a writer who was paid (though often not well) for her work. The second tier was the unassailable fact that I was drawn to the big sky and austere, angular landscape of Nebraska in an almost chemical way.

The way I discovered that sky and landscape was that I went to Lincoln to research a magazine article about female methamphetamine addicts. During the week I was there, I met some impossibly nice people and, moreover, noticed that the cost of living was impossibly low. The way I actually ended up moving there was that I went home to New York, spent more than a year thinking fondly about Nebraska, and eventually woke up one morning realizing I'd rather be waking up on the prairie for $500 a month rent than paying twice as much to face an air shaft. So I called the impossibly nice people and told them I was immigrating to their exotic land. They were delighted, if utterly bewildered. They told me to stay with them—they had a farm, no less—as long as necessary while I found my own place. So a few months later I gave notice on my apartment, packed up my stuff, threw myself a going-away party, and left town. And from the moment the plane touched down on the tarmac—a vast Great Plains tarmac that seemed to spread out for miles in all directions—I knew I'd done, if not necessarily the smart thing, an unequivocally right thing.

I'd wriggled my way out of the city's imperious grip. To my greater elation, though, I was in house heaven.

From my New York perspective, the real estate in Lincoln was so affordable it almost seemed free. Grand Arts and Crafts houses of the "prairie school" sold for as little as $150,000, three-bedroom clapboard bungalows for $75,000. I wasn't looking to buy, of course, but just knowing the housing stock was not only appealing and plentiful but also accessible to an ordinary, middle-class person made the world feel suddenly manageable, humane even. I rented the ground floor of a charmingly shabby 1920s-era house for $525 a month. The place had five whole rooms. These rooms included a dining room with gleaming, intricate woodwork and built-in glass cabinetry. French doors divided the living room from my office, and the bathroom had a cast-iron claw-foot tub. Even though the neighborhood, a collection of bungalows and apartment houses adjacent to the aforementioned professorial region, was not exactly Lincoln's most affluent—many a sofa could be spotted on a front porch—I found myself giddy. For the first time in years, paying the rent and the electric bill did not invite a panic attack. For the first time ever, people around me were simply living their lives rather than pulling themselves up. And although I was still too much my parents' child to completely abandon my lifelong class ascendancy mission (I still called editors in New York and chased writing assignments; in my Cynthia Rowley heels I was still a pretentious twit some of the time), I found myself reclining into some version of serenity. I drank beer on the porch. The sound of train whistles made my cheeks flush.

Naturally, I met a guy. An artist/landscaper/aging slacker. I moved with him to the countryside, where we rented a house whose porch was sagging to one side like some sad drawing in

a children's book. The house sat on ten acres of pasture surrounded by hundreds of acres of corn and soybean fields:
an actual little house on the actual prairie. This thrilled me
beyond comprehension. I began and eventually finished a
novel about a girl who moves to a fictional Midwestern town.
The girl in the book would also move to a farmhouse, but she
would move into a *large* farmhouse with multiple bedrooms
and a mudroom with wainscoting, wide-planked floors, and
weather-beaten windows on three sides. The real-life version
was a four-room saltbox with bedrooms scarcely big enough
for beds. We painted the walls in aquamarines and periwinkle
blues and filled the place with antiques and pieces of stained
glass. We got rocking chairs for the porch and a floppy-eared
puppy we named Rex. We drank together too much and spoke
to each other too little. The rent was $700.

Though I harbored an often irrational fondness for this
guy—despite having no discernible income or employment, he
was handsome and hilarious and a good cook—I didn't move
in with him because I thought we'd be together forever. I
moved in with him because I knew there was practically *no
way* we'd be together forever. I realize that's just the kind of
mind-set that's contributing to the moral decay of America; I
know that's why the terrorists hate us. But there you go. I
moved in with him because at that point in my life the thing
I wanted more than anything else was to live in a farmhouse on
ten acres and, like it or not, such endeavors are best taken on
with a partner. Plus, I loved the guy; that much was true. But
we both knew we were never going to last more than a few
years on that place. You can only sit on your lopsided porch
drinking mediocre wine and eating mediocre Brie from the
Hy-Vee supermarket and staring at the cows across the road
for so long. As it was, I did this for nearly three years.

I'm pretty sure I mean that literally. The way I recall it, one day I was moving into that house and discovering the pleasures of semi-intoxication on that lopsided porch, and the next thing I knew it was more than two and a half years later and I was still sitting there. This is not uncommon in Nebraska.

Not that a part of me wouldn't have loved to stay on that farm—or, better yet, some other farm—forever. In braver moments, I could see myself staking my own claim on the land, wandering alone and wraithlike through some rambling, inexpensive manse. But no matter how vivid these scenarios, I eventually couldn't shake the feeling that it was time to leave the countryside. Although I'd stuck around far longer than I'd ever imagined I would, my final verdict was that remaining on that porch, eating that cheese, would turn the best decision I'd ever made—leaving New York—into the worst one. I may have been rather glamorously tanned and windblown on that gusty, treeless terrain, but I was also always a little hungover.

But where to go? Making a life for myself inside Lincoln city limits was an option, of course. I could have found a sweet house for an even sweeter price. And by now, in addition to the impossibly nice friends with the farmhouse, I had plenty of people to pal around with in town. I went out regularly for lunch and dinner. I ran into acquaintances at the farmers' market. I was even in a book club. But when I closed my eyes and imagined a snapshot of my future self, I just didn't picture the state capitol building or Buzzard Billy's Armadillo Bar and Grillo (of which I was a regular) in the background. This was sad, though sadder yet was that I had no interest in returning to New York either. Even though I half believed that my old friends were still right where I left them, huddled in bars arguing about the state of contemporary fiction and so sure I was coming back that there was actually a drink waiting for me on the table, I couldn't go back. I'd gone soft. I'd become too attached to the acoustics of life in an honest-to-goodness house—especially that piquant, summery sound of a wooden screen door slamming—to go back to clanking elevators and hollering building supers. Besides, the puppy had grown into an eighty-five-pound sheepdog. He couldn't live in New York, at least not comfortably, and by then I'd realized that I couldn't either.

My solution was Los Angeles. I know what you're thinking. A sellout maneuver, an obvious choice, a step backward. But bear with me while I say a thing or two about the place. When you're as predisposed as I am to wanderlust, any activity that occurs outside your own home (walking to the corner store, for instance) is an exercise in looking around and determining whether you'd rather live there than where you're currently living. All foreign and domestic travel, all excursions around the city, all books, movies, and television shows depicting particular locations become fodder for relocation fantasies. It goes without saying that the real estate section of the newspaper is a form of pornography. So, with a few exceptions (Carbondale, Illinois; San Francisco), I think it's fair to say that I've never visited a place without imagining myself permanently or at least semipermanently installed there.

That is to say, I remember at age twenty-six sitting in the unforgiving sun at my brother's graduation from USC and thinking that with a proper hat and sunglass collection, a person could do worse than to live there. I remember being sent to Hollywood a few months later to write a magazine profile of a young woman who competed in mountain bike races with a dead piranha around her neck (why this interview was in Hollywood I can no longer remember; the biker lived in another state) and thinking how nice it was to be able to drive around in an air-conditioned car rather than ride the stinky subway. Of course, I didn't admit much of this at the time. Back then, I was still nursing my adolescent crush on New York, and I often made fun of L.A., decrying it as a cultural wasteland that couldn't hold a match to the gritty wonders of, say, a certain "amazing" borscht restaurant in the East Village. I said those things because I believed that saying those things made you a real New Yorker. And like most people who protest too hard, I ended up going back on everything I'd said and embracing all that I'd disparaged.

It helped, too, that I had friends in L.A., most of whom seemed to be doing remarkably well. Lots of people from Vassar had headed west after graduation and parlayed their black-and-white, 16-millimeter student films into jobs producing reality shows. Additionally, Stephanie, my 100th Street roommate, had moved there a few years after leaving our apartment and immediately began getting noticed as a stand-up comedienne (sometimes telling jokes she'd tossed off while we were conspiring about what to do with Brad). Moreover and most shocking of all, my best friend, Alison, as unwavering a Manhattanite as I'd thought there ever was (like my father, she disliked barbecues on account of the outdoors factor), had ditched New York shortly before my departure for Nebraska to follow a boyfriend to L.A. She even finally learned to drive, though it took her nearly three years and two failed tests and she remained partial to the Santa Monica Big Blue Bus. Still, she adored L.A. She loved it, actually. Although she'd parted ways with the boyfriend a year after the move, she'd always been grateful to him for showing her, as she put it, that "it's possible to go entire weeks without ever being either chilly or too warm."

She had a point. Los Angeles is nothing if not the geographical equivalent of Baby Bear's porridge: not too cold, not too hot, but, rather, a study in the unsung pleasures of lukewarm. I won't lie: conspicuous intellectualism is not L.A.'s racket. When Midwestern kids get on that proverbial Greyhound bus and head for one of the coasts the way my parents should have long ago, the brainy ones tend to go east and the good-looking, not-so-brainy ones tend to go west. You see them strolling, mouths agape, down Hollywood Boulevard or waitressing at Marie Callender's: blue-eyed high-school quarterbacks who were told they should try modeling but will be back home selling cars within six months; corn-fed Iowa kids who were the stars of their school musicals but just might end up in porn. I'm generalizing, of course. There are a million exceptions; this is only half the story. L.A. has more than its share of art-house pontificators, of pallid bibliophiles, of math types. It has major universities and major museums and quite a lot of independent bookstores. But it doesn't wear erudition on its sleeve. Unlike New York, it doesn't mind if you haven't read Mann. It values a nice backyard over the prospect of being neighbors with Thomas Pynchon. Moreover, unlike San Francisco, it doesn't purport to be "evolved." The people of L.A. are honest about themselves and their city. They know it's flawed; they know there's at least one asshole for every decent person; they don't waste their breath telling outsiders how great it is. If San Franciscans are evangelical about their city, always spreading the gospel of its goat cheese and its tolerance and the way the fog descends upon its holy bridge in chiaroscuric rapture, Angelinos are Jewish about theirs. Either you're among the chosen or you're not. Either you get why it's good to live in L.A. or you don't.

There was great appeal in this. Even having never lived there, I recognized the nonpreciousness of L.A. and was drawn to it. So after five years of telling Alison I'd consider moving once I got everything else out of my system, I finally acquiesced. It wasn't hard, really. Not only could I twist the decision around in my mind to make it seem in keeping with the *Little House on the Prairie* motif—they traveled west, after all—but it so happened that for the first time in my life, I had some actual money.

I'd had, as they say in the corporate world, a "liquidity event." I'd sold the novel about the girl who moves to a fictional Midwestern town. To my shock, I'd sold it for enough money that even after I paid off my $80,000 of debt and replaced my twelve-year-old Toyota with a new Subaru station wagon, I had a considerable amount left over. And therein my struggles around deciding where to live began to work in tandem with struggles around deciding whether and where to buy a house. Thus began phase two of my obsession with housing: the nonhypothetical phase.

One characteristic of the nonhypothetical phase is that, thanks to a combination of crippling indecision and my newfound financial cushion, I spent the next two years changing addresses almost as often as I changed the oil in my car. That is to say, as nonhypothetical as things could have been (that is, I could have bought a house right away and been done with things), I was actually living a pretty theoretical existence. Or at least a transient one. As a result, the chronology gets complicated. I'm going to try to lay this out as simply as possible, but if you're still confused, don't feel too bad. I didn't know where I was half the time either.

I had not gone directly to L.A. from the little house on ten acres. Having extricated myself from the relationship with the artist/landscaper/aging slacker in the predictably messy way, I took Rex and went to live with my friend Kimberly in Lincoln.

She owned a well-appointed Cape Cod house in a posh neighborhood near the country club. She was also in the process of deciding whether to remarry her ex-husband, who lived near Los Angeles, so she was only there about half the time.

The four months that I lived in this house were more than a little surreal. Shortly after selling the novel, I also had a movie deal, and I eventually went out to L.A. to meet with the producers and to convince them to let me write the screenplay. I recognize that that's quite possibly one of the most obnoxious sentences ever written but—spoiler alert—this meeting basically amounted to the pinnacle of my Hollywood career. Mostly, this trip was a housing reconnaissance mission. Alison, who lived near the beach in Venice, announced that she'd found the perfect spot for me: Topanga Canyon. This was a magical place, she said (it would be magical for me, anyway; personally she thought the whole place kind of smelled like feet), a hippie–cum–trust funder–cum–wannabe–cowboy enclave in the Santa Monica Mountains, nine miles up a mountain pass off the coast. There were log cabins and tepees as well as eco-friendly/solar-paneled/sustainable/generator-runs-completely-off-of-hemp multimillion-dollar estates. There were writers and artists and corporate lawyers and probably glassblowers who lived in yurts. Moreover, there was land. So much land, in fact, that not only could I probably continue to fan the flame of my farm-girl persona but I'd have to watch out for mountain lions while I was at it. She knew this much because she'd eaten lunch at the Inn of the Seventh Ray, a $30-per-plate vegetarian organic eatery surrounded by sagebrush and Buddha statues just off Topanga's main road, and, having taken a drive through the winding hills afterward, pronounced it, in her inimitable style, "nowhere I'd want to live but just weird enough for you."

Beguiled by the promise of tepees and maybe even artist/ landscapers who weren't aging slackers, I spent the remainder of my trip searching Craigslist for rentals in Topanga Canyon. By the time my plane back to Nebraska took off from LAX, I was holding two separate and shiny keys to my new life. Not only had I fooled the movie producers into giving me a screenwriting deal, but I had a lease on a guest apartment over the garage of a multimillion-dollar house so high in the hills it overlooked thirty miles of coastline. I was set to move in a month.

The timing couldn't have been better. Kim was returning to her ex-husband and selling her house. Since she was also headed for the L.A. area, I could piggyback some of my furniture on her moving truck. The rest of my things (during my time in Nebraska I'd acquired a rather startling amount of early-twentieth-century American furniture) would remain in a storage unit in Lincoln until I had a bigger place someday and could send for them. For the first time in a long time, everything seemed on track.

Then I met Linda the Realtor. She was representing the couple that had bought Kim's house. And since Kim was still in California most of the time, I often found myself chatting with her while she was sitting in the living room waiting on the inspection or attending to some other piece of business. I don't know if it was trepidation about my imminent move or procrastination on the screenplay, but for some reason I began talking to her about how much I'd loved living in the little farmhouse with the lopsided porch (since moving back to town, I'd missed it more than I'd anticipated) and how in many ways I still dreamed of having a big farmhouse. I didn't necessarily see this as a full-time kind of thing, I explained, more of a vacation-house kind of situation. And because Linda needed clients and commissions as much as any Realtor, she did what any decent businesswoman would do. She showed me listings for farms.

You need to understand that I was no stranger to the allure of acreage for sale ("acreage" is the preferred local term for out-of-town land that isn't necessarily a working farm). During my years with the artist/landscaper/aging slacker (who was now my mostly amicable ex), we were as enthusiastic about the idea of buying a farm as my mother had been about Sunday open houses. Never mind that we had no money for one. Never mind that many of the ones we looked at weren't even for sale but just abandoned, tornado-ravaged wooden frames that we imagined ourselves acquiring for nothing and restoring to habitability. I knew from these excursions that the vast majority of out-of-town homesteads were appalling. If they were new, they were usually prefab monstrosities with garages bigger than the houses themselves. More heartbreakingly, if they were old, they'd been raped by "improvements" like dropped ceilings, wall-to-wall carpet, and aluminum siding. It was rare to see something halfway appealing and almost unheard of to see something genuinely exciting.

Hence the saga of the house at Northwest 207th Street and Rural Route G. I'm not sure if I stumbled across the place when I was out driving around with Ex, which we were still apt to do for fun, or if it was on Linda's list of places to show me. In any case, the day I walked inside it was the day my California plans began, if not exactly fading away, losing significant muscle tone. I was ready to head west. I truly was. But as I stood in the driveway with Ex and with Linda, who'd had to rustle up the key from some faraway small-town listing agent, I felt my convictions slipping out from under me. The place bore an uncanny (read: scary and bizarre) resemblance to the

farm I'd invented in my novel. That is to say, it was a rambling, creaking, quite-possibly-not-going-to-make-it-through-
another-winter two-story clapboard house with five bedrooms,
a living room, a dining room, a kitchen, and (to my delight) a
mudroom with wide-planked floors, wainscoting, and windows (weather-beaten, naturally) on three sides. It sat on
about fifteen acres and had several outbuildings, including a
smokehouse, a stable, and a handful of red wooden barns in
various states of dilapidation. One more winter unoccupied
and the place might have been on the way to ruin. Rolling
hills of soybeans and corn undulated in every direction. On
the roof of the largest barn, a weather vane spiked the bound-
less blue sky.

The asking price: $120,000.

"No," I said. "I can't. I'm moving to California."

"Okay," said Ex.

"Okay," said Linda.

On the drive back to town, I was so distracted I nearly
slammed my Subaru into a cow that had wandered into the
gravel road. And that made me cry. Not because I was startled.
But because—I had to admit it—I loved that cow. I loved the
loose gravel and the broken fence that had allowed the cow to
get out and the dust all over the car and the grains of soil
always in my hair. I loved the whole damn hangover that was
Nebraska.

But, no. I was done. I was leaving.

Obviously, I should have flown to California. Thanks to my
infusion of cash, I could have put the car on the moving truck
or had it shipped out without great financial hardship. I could
have swallowed my fear about putting Rex in the cargo hold of
an airplane—to this day, I have vowed *never*—and whisked us
both to our destination in a matter of hours rather than a mat-

ter of endless, conversation-starved, talk-radio-addled days. But when it comes to moving, unless you're crossing an ocean, I believed then as I do now that the only honest mode of transportation is the automobile. You need to see the highway miles unfold before you. You need to take both credit and responsibility for the distance you're covering. You need, upon arrival, to be so tired and so hungry for anything other than gas station food that it doesn't occur to you to be totally freaked-out about the fact that you have no phone number and no idea where the nearest supermarket is.

There are many dramas inherent to relocation via the highway: the tears triggered by a country song, the weird free fall of registering at a motel and not knowing your address, the exhilarating merger of open road and open future. But no one ever talks about those agonizing miles between your departure point and the point at which the interstate fades into a generic ribbon of asphalt. No one ever talks about the suspension of disbelief required to pull out of a driveway that is no longer yours, coast through a neighborhood that will soon no longer be home, and pass—if not for the last time ever, at least for the last time before they become symbols of nostalgia—the landmarks that, while utterly prosaic, have long been the only thing standing between disorientation and sweet familiarity. No one ever talks about the importance of staring straight ahead while making this exit. You cannot turn your head and acknowledge the park, the museum, your favorite restaurant. You cannot wonder if the person driving that red Honda you just passed is your friend from the gym. Like breaking up with a lover, you need to be as gracious as possible, but even more so you just need to walk out. You cannot play Goodnight Moon. You cannot bid farewell to the yellow house on the corner. You cannot duck inside the church and light a candle.

You cannot stop and get coffee. You can only look straight ahead and drive. You can only think about the next thing, the hello and not the goodbye, the up and onward and not the over and out.

Take it from one who did none of the above. Like an addict bargaining for one last fix, I found myself leaving the Lincoln city limits and not merging onto Interstate 80 but continuing south and then turning east (as in, the opposite direction of California) for fifteen miles or so to the farm on Northwest 207th Street and Rural Route G. It wasn't even 6:00 a.m.; the sun was pushing a ridge of pink light across a gray sky, and I had on National Public Radio, though it was too early for even *Morning Edition,* which meant that the overnight host was still playing Berlioz and Wagner and, I suspected, drinking tea and doing crosswords in the dark (I knew this for a fact because I knew her; I also knew she was paid $7 an hour). The coziness of this all—plus the fact that as I came over the hill and saw the farm come into view, I felt that God himself was waiting there with my name on a sign like a limo driver at the airport— was sufficiently distracting that I almost missed the driveway and, as a result, had to slam on the brakes and peel into it in a cloud of dust.

And that's when I knew I had made a terrible mistake. I should have left Kim's house and gotten right on the interstate. Barring that, I should have made a U-turn the minute I hit Northwest 207th. I should have taped a picture of a palm tree on my dashboard and used it as a focal point until these spasms of stupidity passed. But there I was, at dawn, sitting in a Subaru loaded down with computer equipment and blankets and a dog, staring at a farm that I suddenly wanted almost as much as I'd ever wanted anything. I needed to save it from ruin. I was its only hope against the violence of winter—or a buyer with the inevitable bad taste. I got out of the car and let Rex out, too. I kicked the gravel and surveyed the outbuildings, wondering which one might make the best writing studio. I was about to stroll out to the edge of the cornfield to watch the sunrise when, as though I'd touched an electrical fence that divides sanity from insanity, I commanded Rex back into the car, slammed the hatchback, threw myself behind the wheel, and pulled out even faster than I'd pulled in. I got on the nearest entrance to the interstate heading west and didn't so much as look in the rearview mirror for half an hour. Nor did I cry for the entire two-and-a-half-day journey.

To anyone who's considering a move to Southern California, know this: unless you're relocating from Phoenix or Taos or Reno—in other words, from one desert to another—autumn is not the time to answer Hollywood's call. The "perfect" weather is counted among the region's chief commodities. But every year we pay a tariff called September and October. This is the season of fires, of the Santa Ana winds, of ash-choked skies and mercilessly hot, still nights and public radio commentators making endless references to the Raymond Chandler line about meek little wives feeling the edge of a carving knife and studying their husbands' necks. There weren't a lot of fires that first year I was in L.A.—there would be plenty of time for that—but even during that relatively tame fall I was aware of the nearness of a certain unavoidable doom. It wasn't just the threat, infinitesimal yet omnipresent, of a mountain lion bounding from the rocks when I was walking the dog, or of the whole earth being swallowed within seconds by an 8.6 quake. It was the way things that are supposed to be slow, such as erosion, seemed to happen before your eyes. Within hours in California, a hillside can be burned, a road washed out, a house loosened from its foundation and clinging to a slope by only its pipes. And that first autumn, as I waited like a fool for some semblance of October crispness, I don't know what was more unbearable: the fact that the air was so hot that the front door-knob burned my hand or the fact that fall catalogs, with their delicious sweaters and scarves and wool dresses, continued to arrive in the mailbox even though I couldn't possibly order any of it because it was ninety-five degrees on Halloween.

Even after two months in Topanga, even as the days grew short, the over-the-garage apartment, which was totally bereft of shade, baked in the sun like a clay ashtray made by a school-child and permanently forgotten in an art-room kiln. To be above the tree line in the Santa Monica Mountains means that you're often quite literally above the clouds. As though you're in a hot, shadeless heaven—or on an airplane going nowhere—the clouds form a silvery layer beneath you that blocks the view of the land and seems to stop the ocean breezes in their tracks.

The houses, too, are oversized and new and made from materials—glass and sandstone and limestone—from which unforgiving sunlight seems to ricochet and blind passersby. Unlike the rustic A-frames and serene post-and-beams of the lower and mid-canyon, where it was not only cooler but also dark and leafy and oddly redolent of the smell of either tomato soup or marijuana, the peak of the canyon felt craggy and exposed and stripped of natural life.

That's not to say I didn't experience my share of coyotes and deer and other predictable representatives from the California animal kingdom (in my time there I'd see owls and a tarantula, though never a mountain lion). It's just that the threat of fire (barbecues and outdoor smoking were federal offenses) and, especially in the upper reaches of the canyon, the sense that

anywhere you might want to go felt immeasurably far away—
the road from the coast to the village area of the canyon was
nine miles of steep, cliff-hugging switchbacks; the road from
the village to my hilltop apartment was another five miles up a
narrow, flood-prone pass—brought a heightened drama to
minor events. On my second day in the apartment, I stood on
the balcony and watched a helicopter bank around the mountain from the south and draw closer and closer until the
bushes began shaking and dust rose from the ground in cloud-
bursts, and eventually it brushed over me and, astonishingly,
landed in the yard of the large stucco English-manor-style
house across the street. Since this yard was also often used as
a riding ring, a great deal of hay and soil and horse manure
whirled into a cyclone as the helicopter touched down. From
the driveway, where I'd run for a better vantage point, I saw a
woman emerge from the house. She was clutching a baby. A
paramedic jumped out of the helicopter—its blades were still
rotating; its giant metal body made the nearby Land Rover
look like a toy—and ducked his way through the debris until
he caught her elbow and guided them both in. Within seconds
the thing was in the air again, the shrubs were oscillating,
and the dust had formed a curtain down the center of the road.
The helicopter murmured out of the canyon until, like a fly let
out of a window, it was a black dot and then nothing at all.

I remember being shaken up by this scene. I assumed the
baby was unconscious. I was afraid it might even be dead. I
found myself imagining the scene inside that helicopter: a desperate, hysterical mother shouting above the noise, an EMT
who knew it was too late, an infant gone blue.

A few days later, I met a woman who lived a few houses up
the road.

"Oh, that!" she said. "The baby just fell off the bed and was stunned for a minute. Once you call 911, they're required to come out. And since all our evacs are airlifts—well . . . that's just the deal here. The baby was back to normal by the time they arrived, but I guess she took her in to be looked at. Can't hurt, right?"

So this was my new home: a land where babies were carried off in helicopters and the sun seemed so close to the earth you could almost hear it buzzing like a fluorescent light. As for the residents, I'd see them in the general store (which smelled fine to me), wearing yoga pants and giant shawls as they pawed through bins of overpriced fennel. But because of the sleepy, home-oriented culture of canyon life, I never really met any of them. Despite some efforts to wiggle my way into things by driving halfway down the mountain to the coffee shop on Sunday mornings and looking up from my newspaper every four seconds to determine if anyone had walked in who seemed worth talking to (though what does "worth talking to" mean, and, moreover, what good has ever come from sitting in a coffee shop by yourself?), I barely spoke to anyone during my first month in the canyon.

That sort of went for my landlord, too, who I'll call Bill. Though he was well-meaning and distinctly uncreepy (an anomaly, apparently, in single male proprietors of rentable guest apartments in the canyon), he also did not always seem entirely human. A sales rep for a drug company, he'd built the house and adjacent garage/guest unit with insurance money from his original (and ostensibly more modest) house, which had been destroyed in a fire a decade earlier. This must have been quite a settlement, because the new house called to mind a cross between an Ian Schrager hotel and the Getty Center. An austere, modernist slab of limestone and glass, the place was imposing if rather understated on the outside and spotless on the inside. For reasons I couldn't fathom, since he clearly didn't need the money, he rented out two rooms in the house as well as the above-the-garage apartment, though I rarely saw my fellow tenants. In the living room, the mahogany-colored floors gleamed as though covered with a thick layer of nail polish. The kitchen, which contained no traces of food, was lined with granite countertops on which nothing but a shiny black coffeemaker and a toaster—both immaculate enough to suggest lack of use—sat like items in a furniture store display.

Bill's chief companion was his dog, which roamed the hills of the canyon all day and sometimes all night. A Texan (not the Austin kind but the small-town, ranchy kind) of indeterminate age—I put him in his late fifties, but what did I know?—he made occasional reference to an ex-girlfriend but otherwise seemed to have few friends or acquaintances. I assumed that was the reason he had tenants, though his behavior was so frosty I often wondered if he had some kind of Asperger's-like social disorder. He did complicated mathematical calculations to determine how many kilowatt hours of electricity I'd used and presented me with annotated bills. The only laundry area on the premises was inside his house next to the kitchen, and upon my moving in, he proclaimed that until he could trust me enough to give me a key, I'd have to do my laundry only during the day on weekends, when he was home. (One day, weeks later, he knocked on my door and said, verbatim, "I now trust you. Here is a key.")

Bill wasn't in any way an unkind man, just an extraordinarily awkward one. He was also, at least as far as I could tell, extraordinarily sad. In the evenings, as I stood on the balcony of my apartment and watched the sun drop into the gray mirror of the Pacific Ocean, I often glimpsed Bill through his kitchen window. Every night, he'd sit down on a stool at his kitchen counter and eat his dinner with a glass of red wine. What was most striking about this was not only the old-fashioned elegance of the meals—they always appeared to be something like chicken cordon bleu or roast beef with carrots (and not the microwavable kind either)—but also the fact that he ate while staring straight ahead. From my vantage point on the balcony, I saw neither reading material nor the blue glow of a television set. And as I stood there, sometimes drinking black tea if I was going to attempt to motivate myself to leave the mountaintop for the evening, sometimes drinking wine if I needed to let myself off the hook, I often wondered if geographical beauty made loneliness that much more lonely. Was it better to eat dinner alone facing that view? Was it better to silently chew your roast beef while watching the shadows descend onto the cliffs and the sun drop into the sea? Or was eating alone best suited to a double-wide trailer or a moldy studio apartment with a view of a parking lot?

The times I noticed, Bill ate facing away from his windows. So maybe there's your answer.

For my part, I ate facing the computer. And to my great distress, I was using the computer not to write my screenplay or even a new book but to surf the Internet and look at pictures of real estate. I looked at places for sale and for rent. I looked in L.A. and New York and even places I'd never been. I looked at mansions and shacks, studio apartments and penthouses. I looked, of course, at farms in Nebraska. And then I started having the extra-room dream again. As before, the property lines of my life stretched far beyond the place I actually lived. They drew themselves around imaginary houses—bigger houses, zany houses, houses without floors—and taunted me in my sleep. Within days, the extra-room dream expanded to include extra barns, extra cornfields, extra horizons, extra oceans. And though I tried to focus on the present, my mind couldn't keep from snapping back to the farm on Northwest 207th Street and Rural Route G. Within a month of arriving in Topanga, I found myself calling Linda.

"I think I want to make an offer on that place," I told her.

"Okay," she said. This was delivered in precisely the same tone—simultaneously neutral and chirpy—she'd used a month earlier when I'd declared I was permanently leaving Nebraska.

My details on what happened next are fuzzy. I recall that there was quite a bit of faxing back and forth. Since I did not have a fax machine in the apartment and the "business center" at the Topanga general store was apparently operated by someone on a permanent vacation, I found myself driving to a Mail Boxes Etc. some eighteen miles away in the San Fernando Valley to make the bid. Meanwhile, the farm, which was unoccupied, seemed suddenly to be both for sale and not for sale. There was also some confusion as to who the actual owner was. Such murkiness is not uncommon in rural real estate transactions. Often the person selling the property is doing so on behalf of an aging parent, and even more often that parent is disappointed that his or her offspring is not keeping the place and farming the land himself or herself, a dynamic that sets up a teeter-tottering climate of guilt and resentment and therefore causes a house to be simultaneously on and off the market.

But in the case of Northwest 207th Street and Rural Route G, I'm almost certain what was happening was that the sellers were cognizant of the one factor in this equation I'd

chosen to ignore, namely that I was wholly incapable of managing a farm and would likely not save it from winter's ruin but
rather hasten its journey there. How could they possibly have
thought differently? This was a tiny rural community in which
the median home price was about $50,000 and there were
hardly any unmarried people, let alone single women with *Little House on the Prairie* fixations. And now, after having the
place on the market so long that they'd nearly forgotten about
it, the sellers were being told that a thirty-two-year-old woman
who'd once lived in New York City but was now living on a
mountaintop in Los Angeles wanted to buy it with money
she'd earned from writing a book. Moreover, this woman
planned to live there on a part-time basis.

They rejected my offer of $99,999.

Undeterred, I countered with $110,000. In truth, "coun-
tered" may not be the right word here. I'm not sure the sellers
responded to my original offer with an actual number; it may
have been something closer to a no. But from my makeshift
workstation in that cubelike apartment, I developed a relationship to my desktop calculator that was almost stalkerlike
in its intensity. Now that I'd been thwarted, I wanted the farm
even more, in no small part because I remained convinced
that whoever bought it would assault it with carpet and wallpaper and granite kitchen islands from Home Depot and that
it was up to me—the caped crusader of good design, the
preservationist of the prairie—to save it from this fate. I still,
however, had no plans to live there year-round, a consideration
that made my price point a significantly more complicated
equation. I needed, in other words, to be able to pay for an
apartment in L.A., plus afford the mortgage on the farm, plus
pay whatever it would cost to hire someone to take care of the
farm when I wasn't there (and let's face it, even when I was),

plus whatever it would cost to travel back and forth between California and Nebraska. Having absolutely no idea what any of this would cost, I'd find myself losing focus on the numbers on the calculator and instead drifting into a fantasy wherein I'd be strolling through the prairie grass that surrounded the house, the wind blowing my suddenly long and improbably lustrous hair behind me and whispering "owner."

The seller refused the $110,000 offer. I came back with $120,000. Considering that this was the asking price, I figured we were done.

"They've accepted another offer," Linda told me.

"What?" I shrieked. "For how much? From whom?"

"A hundred and ten thousand dollars," she said. "They sold it to a friend."

No doubt I spent several minutes sputtering about how unfair this was and insisting that it couldn't possibly be legal and what the hell were they thinking and what kind of people would accept an offer that's *less* than what someone else was willing to pay, especially someone who'd be putting *at least* 20 percent down and who (and I'd told Linda to impress upon them my love for early-twentieth-century American antiques) would restore the place to its original turn-of-the-century rustic splendor rather than install the wall-to-wall bedroom carpet and Jenn-Air-equipped, faux-marble-tiled kitchen that this "friend" (no doubt the proud owner of a NASCAR driver-of-the-month wall calendar) probably had up his or her crappy poly-blend sleeve. No doubt I asked if there was any way to save the situation. Couldn't they be made to reconsider? Wasn't there a way to supply some sort of additional proof of my wonderfulness? Did they know I had a novel coming out?

No doubt Linda was kind and conciliatory and told me there were lots of farmhouses out there and that she'd keep looking for me. And while, thinking back on it, I'm not sure I really ranted out loud about NASCAR calendars, not to her anyway, the truth is that I don't really remember what I said. The truth is that when I heard this news, I was swept up in a tidal wave of despair that, oddly enough, I can still only compare to the singular pain of being dumped in high school by my first boyfriend. As is nearly always the case with first "loves," the heartache was as profound as it was unwarranted, and as I contemplated the loss of Northwest 207th Street and Rural Route G, all I could think was that I was experiencing a level of devastation that I assumed I'd long ago inoculated myself against as though it were chicken pox.

But there it was again, as raw and as wretched as it had been the first time. Like all events that feel tragic despite clearly being nontragic, losing the farm engendered a pain that was only intensified by the knowledge that I shouldn't have been nearly as upset as I was. But even in the midst of it, I knew the wound wasn't existential so much as it was (embarrassingly, prosaically) personal. It was irksome enough that the sellers had accepted an offer that was $10,000 less than mine (not a small amount in rural Nebraska) and therefore rejected not just my money but, quite literally, me as a person (in their view, *I* was the unsuitable owner: What myopia! What obtuseness! Perhaps there was even sexism at work). The real anguish, however, came from the fact that I could no longer soothe my loneliness by clinging to the fantasy of the farm. As though Northwest 207th Street and Rural Route G had been a life raft in the vast, disorienting sea of my new life in California, I'd clung to its more fantastical qualities for the better part of two months. Suddenly disabused of them, I felt naked and miserable and robbed of my dream. Worse, I felt robbed of the person I'd desperately wanted to be. That person, I'd come to realize in a short period of time, was not the sort who lived over a pharmaceutical salesman's garage in the moneyed, parched crevices of the Santa Monica Mountains. She was the sort who made her own way, who staked her own claim. The problem was that I no longer had any idea where that claim should be.

I'd like to say that I finally picked myself up and made peace with my surroundings, which really should have been visually spectacular enough to counteract whatever dip was occurring in my serotonin levels. I'd like to say that I buckled down and threw myself into the screenplay or started a new novel or even wrote a magazine article or two. Obviously, the happy ending to this story would be that I met some impossibly sexy glass-blower (who was both a real artist *and* commercially success-ful) and moved with him into a luxury yurt. However, this was not to be. As I'd so often done in the wake of my torpor at Vas-sar, I spent my time not reading or writing or helping those less fortunate but riding the miserable pendulum that swings between the impulse to try to make things work and the impulse to escape.

I began taking yoga classes at the Topanga yoga studio (the community might not have had a fax machine, but you better believe it had yoga). On Friday nights, when there was live music at the local bar and grill, I drove halfway down the mountain and planted myself on a bar stool. In neither of these settings did anyone talk to me. Even after I'd attended yoga no fewer than ten times and forced myself to go to the bar no fewer than five times (not including two lamentable din-ners alone there while pretending to read a magazine), I still hadn't met anyone who could have come close to being described as an acquaintance. Even Rex, who spent his days running around the property like a wild thing, seemed keener to hole up in Bill's house in the evenings than in the apartment. Later I would learn that this was because Bill was wooing him with canned dog food (I only fed him dry), but at the time it only added to my suspicion that I'd become an invisible, perhaps even silent and odorless person. At stop signs I took an extra pause before proceeding. Did other cars even see me? Was it possible that in trying to blend into my surroundings I'd somehow erased myself?

Four months after arriving in Topanga, I decided I had to move. Determined to leave the canyon but still unwilling to commit to a lease longer than a few months, I sublet a cottage apartment a few blocks from the beach in Venice. The woman living there, a late-twenty-something named Dani, needed to return to the East Coast for a few months to take care of her mother, who was sick with cancer. The place was furnished, which meant I'd need to put my bed and my other large items into yet another storage unit. But I was by then so desperate to live someplace where running out for milk did not necessarily feel like crossing the Donner Pass—plus Alison lived nearby— that I overlooked the fact that the cottage smelled vaguely like kitty litter.

Amid copious apologies for the inconvenience I was causing, I told Bill that I was moving.

"I won't miss you, but I'll miss Rex," he said.

A few days before Christmas of that year, I moved into Dani's cottage in Venice.

I need at this juncture to say a few things about single women and furniture. You know the self-loathing impulse that causes women who hate their bodies to buy oversized, overly trendy, and cheap clothing? You know that tortured promise we make to ourselves in the dressing room of Target that this will be the last time we buy an ugly skirt for $12 because we're planning to lose weight and *then* we'll invest in a real wardrobe? Multiply that phenomenon by twenty and you have the tragedy of the single woman who won't buy decent furniture because she's waiting until she gets married.

Often this woman's furniture is made of wicker (not including the ubiquitous halogen torchiere lamp); other times it's composed of lightly stained pine of the sort that's frequently used for futon frames and collapsible bookshelves. As with the Target skirt, the bad furniture is almost always provisional. As soon as true love—and a corresponding mortgage—are reeled in, the wicker and pine will be traded in for items from proper furniture retailers. In the meantime, however, the only things for which the single woman will willingly overpay are scented candles. She will have loads of them: fat and thin, pear scented and vanilla scented and "rain" scented, in every imaginable color and shape. The reason she has these is that she believes they will make men want her. She believes that if a guy she likes is in her apartment—even if he's not attracted to her in the least—the singular act of touching a lit match to a slab of wax that smells vaguely like Febreze will alter the chemistry of the encounter in her favor. It will make him lust for her, then fall in love with and marry her.

Dani had her share of candles. She also had a lot of pine furniture. An enormous media cabinet, carved with a floral design and bursting with heavy, overstuffed drawers, dwarfed the living room wall. A sofa blocked a window. The queen-sized bed with its tower of pillows and oddly protruding dust ruffle left only a small strip of walkable space in the bedroom. The aforementioned kitty litter smell, I soon determined, was actually the result of poop from Dani's Yorkshire terrier that had never been picked up off the concrete patio. I was paying $1,600 a month for a three-month lease.

And I was elated to be back in action—or at least within walking distance of a pizza parlor. As odorous and as crowded as Dani's apartment remained even after a series of strenuous cleaning and reorganization efforts, I felt as invigorated as I'd been when I finally left Vassar for good. Alison lived just a few blocks away, and we went to yoga classes together and threw catty dinner parties at her condo. I explored corners of the region—Silver Lake, Palos Verdes, Long Beach—that from a Topanga perspective had seemed outrageously far away but in fact adhered to the standard L.A. travel time metric: twenty-five minutes without traffic, two-plus hours with.

I even finally glued my butt to Dani's wicker desk chair and wrote the screenplay. Miraculously, it did not suck. I know it didn't suck because the agent and the producer both pronounced it "the best effort from a first-time screenwriter I'd ever seen" and declared that I was going to have "a big career" in Hollywood. Translated from film industry b.s. into English, that means "doesn't suck." I got sent on a meeting or two, which is what you do in the entertainment business when you want to sell someone an idea. The meetings were productive in that I learned the best driving routes to Beverly Hills and got to walk around on studio lots but rather pathetic for one glaring reason: I had no ideas, for sale or otherwise. I had no sitcom idea, no romantic comedy idea, no reality show concept.

What I had instead were many, many thoughts about scented candles. There among the bittersweet emanations of Dani's bachelorette paraphernalia, I began to worry for myself. Actually, I began to feel afraid. The fear had something to do with loneliness, but it wasn't entirely about being alone. It was about being alone with awful furniture. It was about growing older and not letting your apartment age alongside you. Looking at Dani's bookshelf, which sagged with diet books and dating books and meditation books and Sarah McLachlan CDs and printed programs from weddings she'd attended years earlier, I was reminded once again that there were worse things than being in your thirties and having no idea when—or if—you were going to meet the person with whom you'd settle down and invest in a decent dining table. Worse was not buying the dining table yourself. Worse was having no real books on your shelf. Worse was having a home that reflected your desperation like a distorting mirror. Dani, like so many other women, wasn't living as much as she was waiting around.

Where was I in this? I was no Dani, that's for sure. How did I know? For one thing, my dog was large and docile, not small and presumably yappy like the varmint that had crapped all over the patio. For another thing, my furniture was generally made of oak, not pine. Granted, it was now divided among two storage units, one in Lincoln and one in the bowels of the San Fernando Valley, where the items I'd brought to Topanga had been carted away when I defected from Bill's guest apartment. But at least I did not own a media cabinet the size of a truck. As for the other ways in which I was not like Dani, as deeply as I could feel them, I began to wonder if, to the outside world, the two of us were virtually indistinguishable. After all, my most intimate companion was my dog. My friends were scattered all over the country, and my immediate family—I spoke on the phone to my mother every two weeks, to my father every two months, and almost never to my brother—was as disparate as ever. I did not, in other words, know what the hell I was doing with myself.

As for who did know what she was doing with herself, or at

least where she was going? That would have been Dani. Per the agreed-upon schedule, she and her terrier were coming back home in a few weeks. I had no home at all.

I could, of course, have easily found a new place to live. There were neighborhoods beyond the scrubbed and shiny stretches of Venice and Santa Monica, neighborhoods where properties— for rent and for sale—were more affordable and in many cases more interesting (if less tempered by ocean breezes) than places like Dani's. They were east of the 405 freeway, east of Hollywood, and I was eager to explore them. But somehow I still wanted to go farther east than that. I wanted to go east of the Rockies. Despite everything I thought I knew about my own needs and proclivities, despite my desire to "be con- nected" (that is, not live in Topanga Canyon), I found myself wanting to go back to Nebraska. Maybe I felt strange about the idea of my novel, which took place in the made-up town of Prairie City, unleashing itself upon the world while I was living somewhere other than the prairie. Or maybe I was just exhausted from the sheer labor of navigating a new city. Chronic lostness was not a malady to be underestimated. On more outings than not, I was forced to drive with *The Thomas Guide* balanced in my lap. Exiting any given freeway ramp, I'd often turn south when I meant to go north or vice versa. Since I had come to L.A. six months earlier, my life had been reduced to an endless effort to make a U-turn.

Was it any surprise, then, that I chose that moment to take a trip back to Nebraska? Sure, there were reasons—a friend's birthday that weekend, not to mention the Haymarket Art Walk, in which another friend was exhibiting her stained glass—but these were nothing particularly to write home about, much less fly halfway across the country for. But suddenly my need to be there was urgent, and the punch of the plane wheels touching down on the Lincoln runway felt like a tranquilizer. I checked in to a bed-and-breakfast on a Thursday and spent a few days visiting old friends (the impossibly nice farm folks, the book club ladies, Ex and his motley associates) and haunting old haunts (the blues bar, the Armadillo Bar and Grillo, various front porches). Then on Sunday morning I met Ex for breakfast, after which we decided to take a drive out to the country. The purpose of this jaunt was twofold: I wanted to drive past the prairie shack we'd once occupied (Ex had by now moved into a $300-a-month two-bedroom apartment with a sunporch) to see whether the new tenants had let it fall into the disrepair that's pretty much par for the course with rural rentals. I also wanted to check out a farmhouse that the *Lincoln Journal Star* had listed as on the market for $157,000. It wasn't that I had designs on it or anything; I just wanted to take a peek.

If only the car had broken down. If only Ex and I had gotten into a screaming match over some long-ago grievance and I'd returned to my B and B, planted myself in the parlor, and drowned my sorrows in hot chocolate and outdated issues of *Audubon* magazine. If only I hadn't called my mother for advice and she hadn't said, "That woodwork sounds terrific, I say go for it," I would not have done what I did. But as it was, I did what I did and so much more. I walked into that farmhouse, beheld its gleaming maple floors, untouched vintage woodwork, built-in glass cabinetry, and kitchen that was miraculously unruined by "updates," and started fishing for my checkbook. In less than ten minutes, I'd made a verbal offer. By the end of the afternoon, I'd made a written one. By the next day, I was in escrow. Ex should have stopped me, of course. But he didn't. He only said, "Well, the floors *are* nice."

The reason these things had been able to transpire so quickly was that the seller of the farmhouse, a warm, intelligent-seeming woman who (naturally) had inherited it but didn't want it, happened to be standing in the house when I walked in and screamed "Oh my God, the floors!" with an enthusiasm unheard of in actual Nebraskans. She had not, it turned out, retained the services of a Realtor, and when I suggested that we consider doing business on our own, thereby eliminating the commission, knocking down the purchase price, and avoiding various bureaucratic headaches, she said, "That sounds fine to me." She then accepted my offer of $150,000 (why it didn't occur to me to try to offer less I do not know), and I made a good-faith deposit of $300. (Depending on where you live in the country, I know these numbers might look like typos. Where, you're wondering, is the other zero? The other zero is the temperature in Nebraska five months a year.)

We then filled out some papers she'd downloaded off the Internet, signed them, and took them to a notary. The escrow period would be the standard thirty days, but I was so excited about occupying the property that I arranged to rent it from her until the closing date. I then flew back to California, packed up my stuff, and turned around and drove to Nebraska.

You may be imagining this farm as some sort of pristinely rustic spread straight out of the movie *Giant* or a Willa Cather novel or, at the very least, the Sundance catalog. Chances are you're thinking that the place must have knocked my socks so far off my feet that they landed somewhere in Iowa. Why else would I, a mostly stable if not always entirely practical person, engage in such a rash series of moves? Did I feel somehow ordained? Did a bearded face appear in the clouds over the soybean fields on that bitter March day and telepathically

inform me that the key to personal happiness, professional ful-
fillment—and maybe even a spread about my novel in *People*
magazine—lay in purchasing this property?

No and no. For one thing, this farm, despite its gymnasium-
like floors and to-die-for woodwork, was no Northwest 207th
Street and Rural Road G. Only ten minutes from downtown
Lincoln, it was more like a regular house that happened to be
surrounded by farmland, its only outbuildings a corroded stable and a newish aluminum shed where the farmer who leased
the crop fields kept his equipment. Though the road was suit-
ably countrified in that it was unpaved (a necessity as far as I
was concerned), Interstate 80 was less than a mile away and,
though I somehow hadn't noticed during that Sunday afternoon open house, fully audible. The drone of 18-wheel trucks
could, it seemed, be heard approaching from ten miles out
and then trailing off ten miles into the distance. In the meantime, the heating vents were caked so thick with dust that to
turn on the furnace was essentially to set off a cyclone of soot
inside the house. The tap water, for its part, was an alarming
shade of yellow green.

The house had four bedrooms upstairs and one downstairs,
plus a living room, dining room, large kitchen, and basement.
My Lincoln storage unit contained my beloved rocking chair,
several boxes of books, some random straight-back chairs, a
few pieces of very large, very old stereo equipment (yes, the
same equipment that I'd dragged, fully hooked up, across the
Vassar quad years earlier), and a number of framed art posters
that my mother had bequeathed to me when she sold Jones
Lane and that I'd never hung up anywhere. Even after I moved
these items into the farmhouse, the place echoed like a scary
underground parking lot in a movie in which some innocent
girl gets stabbed while walking to her Pontiac.

So I went out and bought more stuff. Not just any stuff, but farm stuff. A wood kitchen table painted bottle green. A long schoolteacher's desk. A set of yellow ceramic bowls. It so happened that I was the rightful owner of not just my handmade queen-sized cherrywood bed, which was now in storage in California, but also two additional antique beds: a carved maple three-quarter I'd slept in throughout childhood and adolescence that had been passed down along my father's side of the family; and a cast-iron full-size that, via a set of bizarre and possibly journalistically unethical circumstances, had been shipped to me gratis when I wrote a magazine article about the female obsession with finding the perfect bed. Both of these beds had been in my mother's attic in New Jersey. As a housewarming present she shipped them out to the farm, where I found myself in the extraordinary position of deciding into which two of the five bedrooms I should install them. Having chosen the larger, front-facing upstairs bedroom as my office, I put the cast-iron bed in the other front room and the maple bed in a back room that faced the cornfields (and, distressingly, the aluminum shed) to the south. I made them up with linens I'd picked up at Bed Bath & Beyond and spent alternate nights in each. I was like a lonely, crazy princess in a vast, echoing castle. By day, I scoured antiques shops and waited for various Culligan technicians to come out and test and retest the water. By night, I lay in one of my two beds, wincing at the sound of the interstate and wondering how much it would cost to rent a place in Los Angeles and travel back and forth between the generic paradise of the West and the paradise—at once so addictive and so disappointing—I'd constructed out of Nebraska.

That, after all, was the idea. As had been the case with the ill-fated Northwest 207th Street and Rural Route G, my plan was to use the farm as a sort of low-rent vacation home, the idea being that I'd be on vacation at least as often as I was not on vacation and, even then, it wouldn't technically be vacation since I'd be engaged in very serious writing or reading or interior decorating. In fact, my ultimate plan for Northwest 207th Street and Rural Route G had been to turn it into an artists' colony. Thanks to its outbuildings, which could have been converted into painting studios and little writing huts with relatively little work, I'd allowed myself to concoct an elaborate scenario wherein I was the proprietor of one of the greatest— or at least most picturesque in a minimalist way—creative work centers west of the Mississippi. From Manhattan coke snorters to studio art majors from the University of Nebraska, every stripe of writer and painter and choreographer would convene at my farm for hours of uninterrupted work by day and scintillating repartee by night. So popular would the enterprise become that I'd eventually be able to hire someone to manage it year-round, leaving me free to drift in and out from my L.A. base like a legendary actor in an occasionally recurring sitcom role. In the meantime, of course, I'd be tax-exempt because I'd be running a nonprofit organization. I'd also probably get written up in a *New York Times* arts feature that would show me presiding over a candlelit gazebo supper and describe me as the George Plimpton of the prairie.

Gallingly, however, this farm was not suitable for an artists' colony. Not only were there too few outbuildings; the grounds were unremarkable, the number of acres paltry to the point of being yardlike, and any sense of exotic remoteness undone by the fact that a development of split-level houses was going up at warp speed less than a mile down the road. So, having come to terms with the property's exterior limitations, I tried to focus on its inner beauty. There was, for instance, something incred-

ibly gorgeous and satisfying about the way the upstairs landing
was almost a room unto itself. To reach the top of the stairs,
which made a graceful, lanky turn at a leaded-glass window,
was to come upon the kind of space that seemed to encapsu-
late everything I loved about farms, about the Midwest, about
life itself. No fewer than two hundred square feet, the landing
had walls that were painted a shade of pink so pale it was
almost as if early morning light were perpetually casting itself
on the thick plaster and thicker woodwork. A built-in linen
closet with heavy drawers, tarnished brass handles, and a cabinet latch that clicked shut with that perfect alto timbre
known almost exclusively to early-twentieth-century-era door
hardware took up most of one wall. The floors, of course, were
the same glassy wood that covered the rest of the house.

What excited me most about the landing, though, was the
marrow of all that it meant to be—and to have—a landing.
The fact that a space large enough to be a room was actually
not a room but a portal to other rooms, the fact that not two or
three but *four* other rooms jutted out from this mother ship to
form magical worlds filled with the promise of nighttime reading and snug, windy nights under patchwork quilts—that was
nothing short of delectable. Why was I so stirred? To this day,
I can't quite say. Maybe it was all those years in New York City
apartments with their entrails-shaped hallways and sorry
excuses for "rooms"; maybe it was the collective claustropho-
bia of the prairie shack and then the apartment in Topanga and
then Dani's hamster cage of a cottage. Maybe my small living
spaces had induced a sort of psychological cramping; maybe
my acquisition of this farm was not a deliberate act but an
involuntary reflex, a yawn and stretch writ large.

Whatever it was, though, it was looking increasingly as if it
did not extend beyond the landing. True, the kitchen engaged

me somewhat, particularly the vaguely Cézanne-like effect I could achieve by placing a single apple in the yellow ceramic bowl I'd assigned to the center of the bottle green table. But even if I had been able to drift from set piece to set piece and call it a real life, this house just didn't have the goods. For every thing that was right about it, there were two things that were wrong: a hideously redone bathroom, suspicious cracks in the basement joists, and, of course, that regrettable aluminum shed. There was also, as it happened, the increasingly not-so-minor matter of the water. Even after visits from three different Culligan men, the water ran brown from the faucets even when turned on for ten minutes or longer. This meant buying large plastic jugs of drinking water at the truck stop a few miles down the road and refilling them with clean tap water whenever I happened to be in town. One afternoon, I found myself filling up in a sink in the restroom of the public library. A homeless woman (yes, even Lincoln has them) walked in, wearing a filthy knapsack and dragging a bursting trash bag behind her. She looked me up and down and shook her head.

A reasonable person (who at the very least would have been working with a Realtor and, were she genuinely reasonable, wouldn't have gotten in this situation to begin with) would have bailed out right about this time. A reasonable person would have called the seller and said, "Sorry, can't do this," and vamoosed as fast as possible. I, however, was not scoring high on the reasonable index at that time. With less than two weeks before the close of escrow, I focused my energies not on extricating myself from this mess but rather on making it larger and more complicated.

Because so what if my enthusiasm was waning? The part-time residency plan was still in effect; I just needed to keep my eyes on the bicoastal (semi-coastal?) lifestyle prize. As if a farm in Nebraska were no different from a Greenwich Village apartment for which subletters could be secured on a moment's notice, I'd convinced myself that I would divide my time between there and California. Since summers in Nebraska are as inhumanly hot as the winters are cold, I planned to spend the spring and fall seasons at the farm while returning to Los Angeles for November through March as well as July and August. I would need a car in both places, of course, so this plan involved a four-times-a-year drive across the plains and over the Rockies, which, I reasoned, would give me an opportunity to meditate, or at least listen to a lot of books on tape.

As crazy as everyone thought this plan was, it made brilliant sense to me at the time, not least of all because I oozed commitment phobia from every pore. And provided I could find a way to be gone as much if not more than I was there, the farmhouse would be the ultimate long-distance relationship. I wouldn't be living in it as much as I'd be cooing to it over the phone late at night. I wouldn't be married to it, but, rather, keeping it on the side like a backstreet lover. And true to my phantasmagoric self-image as a mysterious prairie lady who's desired by everyone but can be possessed by no one, it was easy to tell myself that this setup, while crazy, was also authentic.

The more I doubted myself, the more "reasons" for the purchase I came up with. The farm, I told my friends and family, was an investment, "an IRA I can live in" (suddenly I was trotting out the jargon, a real wheeler-dealer). Until I could get the artists' colony up and running, I'd rent it out to visiting professors. I would make it available as a location for movie shoots. I contacted the university and was told there was a hiring freeze.

I called my friend who ran the state film office, and she told me the only movie scheduled to be shot in Nebraska that year was an independent with no location budget. I met with a rental agent, who told me that if I installed a dishwasher and a ceiling fan, she could maybe get $800 a month for it. When I mentioned that the ideal tenant would be someone who only needed it for a few months at a time, she looked at me as if I'd arrived on a nonstop flight from Jupiter. When I started asking around town if anyone knew of a handyman/overseer type of person who could look after the place during the months when I was gone—possibly for free, possibly living there when I was away and then vacating when I returned (unless I could turn the aluminum shed into guest quarters)—I got a lot of blank stares. "Didn't you move to California?" a mechanic I knew from the blues bar shouted to me over the music during happy hour one Friday. "I thought you blew this joint forever! I can't keep you straight."

Funny, I could no longer keep myself straight either. I was buying a property that was so beyond my ability to physically or financially manage that I'd actually begun investigating ways to rent it out before I even owned it. I was also buying a property that I really only liked for its upstairs landing. A week or so before the close of escrow, Rex needed to go out in the middle of the night, and I, sleepless, went with him. The grounds were damp with melting snow, and the air had that dry cough texture that Midwestern air so often has in the late winter. And in that motionless, rawboned air I could hear the interstate as loudly as if I were standing on the shoulder with a flat tire.

When I imagine what it might be like to marry the wrong person, to lie in bed on your wedding night and stare at the crack in the ceiling that, in the space of twenty-four hours, has suddenly come to represent the permanent fissure you've installed in your own life, I imagine that acreage. Its wrongness hit me in the face like a violent gust from the north. I had to turn away; horribly, there was nowhere to turn that wasn't facing either the aluminum shed or the jilted house itself. I closed my eyes. I stared down at the dirty snow. I was thirty-three years old. The number of houses and apartments I'd rented in my adult life far exceeded the number of boyfriends I'd had. It probably even rivaled the number of expensive shoes I'd ever owned. It was there, in the light of a waning, ragged moon and underscored by the whine of not-so-distant trailer trucks, that I came to an understanding that even a schoolgirl would have been quicker to perceive: I didn't want to buy a house; I wanted to shop for a house. I hadn't fallen in love with this house, merely the view from the top of its stairs.

I'm not proud of any of this. On the shame index, my involvement with this property ranks just below the Brad incident. The next day, I reneged on the deal. The seller, who seemed honest and well-meaning and whose name I can no longer remember, probably because I've blocked it out, was so angry she could barely speak. I can still hear the ice in her voice when I told her I was backing out. I can still hear the silence that greeted my profuse apologies. I can feel the knot in my stomach as I dialed the phone and the rush of both humiliation and relief when the call was over. I lost my $300 deposit (the irony that the term for this fee was "good faith" or "earnest" money and that I had failed on both accounts wasn't lost on me), plus, in an effort not to get sued, a few hundred dollars of legal fees to an attorney I should have hired in the first place.

With my novel less than six weeks from publication and much of the spring and summer taken up with book-related travel, I saw no reason to return to L.A. just yet. I went back to the classifieds of the *Lincoln Journal Star*, found a small red-brick ranch house in town, and signed a lease. I then called a moving company to take my stuff from the farmhouse to the ranch house. It was the fourth time in six months that I'd employed movers.

Twenty-four hours before I mailed the keys back to the seller, a photographer from *People* magazine came out and took pictures of me strolling around the prairie grass near the farmhouse. One of these photos appeared next to a review of my novel, and I'm pretty sure it was supposed to convey the idea that I actually lived on the farm. I had no fewer than twenty-five conflicting feelings about the situation; they ranged from guilt that I was being misleading about my living quarters to a secret (though also guilty) thrill in the notion that even if my friends and family knew my rural posture was more or less rigged up, the readers of *People* might think I really did spend my days contemplatively flouncing around my own patch of verdant badlands. Mostly, though, I felt sad. After trying so hard to transform this particular fantasy into a truth, after hurling myself halfway across the country and back in an effort to find the sweet spot between my ideal self and a self I could actually manage and maintain on a daily basis, I'd come up short again. I'd aimed for the hero's journey and instead ended up with a farce. I'd meant for my life to resemble a vast Wyeth landscape, and instead it looked like a snapshot on Dani's shelf. I'd wanted to be special but was turning out to be ordinary. This felt like nothing less than total surrender.

All that said, I loved that the redbrick ranch house had central air-conditioning and a dishwasher. On aesthetic principle, I was generally opposed to this type of domicile—it had awful gold-plated light fixtures throughout and pink floral wallpaper in the bathroom, and one of the two bedrooms was covered in white shag carpet—but after the disorder of Dani's place and then the ocher-colored water of the farm it felt like a sanctuary. I set up the cast-iron bed in the carpeted bedroom—"for guests," I told myself—and somehow never got around to assembling my wooden childhood bed in the other room, so I simply slept on the mattress on the floor, college-style. My book came out, and I spent about a month traveling around the country giving readings (often to sparse crowds that appeared to have shown up primarily for the refreshments). Always with these readings, I had the feeling that the farmhouse in the novel was not one I'd invented but, rather, the lost acreage at Northwest 207th Street and Rural Route G. By midsummer I had returned to the ranch house. The next few months were spent happily reclined in the easy chair that is life in Lincoln—hanging out with Ex, going to meetings of my book club, finding myself tipsy by 6:30 p.m. When, one night, I found myself tipsy by 5:30, I knew it was time to leave again. I called the movers, swallowed the $800 security deposit I'd lost by breaking the lease, and prepared to set out for California again and for good.

Something wrested my emotions on my last night in town. I remember that I'd gone out to dinner with Ex. And then we ended up stopping by a house where there was a party. I can't recall exactly what we were doing there. I think Ex might have been picking up or dropping off something from whoever lived in the house, though in retrospect that makes no sense because in that case we would have been invited. In any case, I didn't go into the party, but sat in the car in the driveway for five or so minutes as Ex dashed inside. The house was a large 1920s-era American Foursquare not unlike my childhood house on Jones Lane, and though the bulk of the party was going on in the backyard, enough people were dribbling out to the front porch and around to the side yard that I could see the general mix. It was kids—mainly youngish teenagers—and adults alike, and I wondered if this was a graduation party, though it was August and really too late in the summer for that sort of thing. Decked out in sandals and khaki shorts and Barenaked Ladies concert T-shirts and sundresses, men and women in their forties and fifties drank beer and gesticulated largely and stuffed chips into their mouths and leaned against porch railings and patted the dog's head. A few of them I knew from my book club: Patty and Deb, their husbands, Phil and whatever-his-name-was. They smiled easily and laughed even easier, and—this was the thing that got me somehow—their children ran underfoot and ducked around them and asked them questions and endured hair tousling and appeared to be laughing at some of the same jokes and were simultaneously part of and separate from the adult world in a way that I don't think I'd ever seen before coming to Nebraska (maybe it had existed in Austin, but then again maybe it hadn't) and, at that point, was convinced I'd never see anywhere else.

Years later—even as little as one year later—I'd realize that this sort of scene (though it was perhaps less a scene than a mood) was available in all kinds of places among all kinds of people. It is, after all, more common than uncommon for regular folks to behave in regular, authentic ways. And while I wasn't even sure that this mood—if that was the word for it— was real or had anything to do with whatever sum I'd arrived at by watching and adding up the random pieces of humanity on the porch that night, I was suddenly seized by a heartbreaking hypothesis. If I was going to live not just among friends but also among like-minded "peers," I reasoned, I would have to give up the visceral pleasures of drinking beer on front porches. I would have to set up shop someplace less cozy, someplace where you couldn't hear the crickets chirping, someplace where there were no wooden screen doors clattering their way through the summers. If I was going to be in "civilization" (which in this case I was defining as the world in which going to work meant doing something of national relevance and keys could not intentionally be left in car ignitions overnight as they sometimes were in Lincoln), I was going to have to give up hearty laughter on porches. If I was going to live in civilization (and it dawned on me now that I was referring to the very venue my father had pronounced "not quite civilized" so many years earlier), I'd have to give up civilized people. And it was such a devastating notion that it nearly left me breathless, even though I was sitting perfectly still in an unmoving car.

Of course, my logical side knew that my definition of "civilization" was totally ass backward. Civilization (unless you were resigning to the ultimate cliché and talking strictly about sushi and avant-garde theater) was not New York or L.A. or whatever teeny-weeny handful of "world class" cities I associated with not throwing your life away. Civilization was not synonymous with standing a very real chance of encountering a celebrity at Starbucks. It was in the eye of the beholder. It was what you made it. It was—like the view from the top of the stairs in the unpurchased farmhouse or the sound of the elevator lurching down its shaft in my beloved building on West 100th Street—the visceral essence of the parts of your home you hold most dear.

But returning home to the ranch house, which was now empty save those mawkish light fixtures, I found myself in the basement sobbing so hard over the clothes dryer that I literally could not stand up. It was a worse display than even the one I'd unleashed in Topanga after learning I wasn't getting Northwest 207th Street and Rural Route G. There were heaving sobs, jaw spasms, gag reflexes. Back then, I'd merely been denied the prize behind door number one. Now the game was over. And unlike back then, when I hadn't known exactly why I was coming so unglued, I knew exactly what this meltdown was about. It was a bitter pill I could taste even through the hard rain pouring from my face. It was the dirty truth about my relentless search for "domestic integrity." It was this awful fact: you cannot pursue authenticity at the same time you are pursuing fabulousness. You cannot have it both ways. You cannot be the down-home farm girl and the queen of lower Fifth Avenue at the same time. You cannot be Maggie O'Connell (the floatplane-piloting, pixie-haircut-sporting, flannel-shirt-wearing cutie from *Northern Exposure*) and also Carrie Bradshaw from *Sex and the City*. You cannot be Dorothy Parker and also Willa Cather. To attempt to be both of these things is to be not only neither but in fact nothing.

I indulged this grief for twenty minutes or so. Then I took my clothes out of the dryer and went upstairs. And the next morning I got in the car and drove west. This time without detours.

FOUR

For six weeks, I lived in a two-story Spanish Colonial in the foothills of Beachwood Canyon, just below the Hollywood sign. I was dogsitting. The plan was to look after two border collies until their owner, a friend of a friend who was working in New York, "sent for" them (this conjured the nonsensical but nonetheless disturbing image of packing the dogs into steamer trunks), after which Rex and I would have the place to ourselves. This was supposed to happen within a few weeks of my arrival, which is why I was paying $1,450 a month rent, an amount that was too high considering the dog care duties and too low considering the size and location of the house. Perhaps as such, the dogs were never sent for, and I continued to pay rent anyway. I was supposed to be writing articles or thinking up ideas for screenplays or television pilots. But because I found it nearly physically impossible to walk three dogs simultaneously, I often went on three or four separate walks a day, which cut into my writing time significantly.

Speaking of dogs, I'm obliged here to give a little shout-out to Rex. He had grown up to be a large, yaklike creature, and he was unequivocally my favorite thing in the world. I'd had pets growing up, but they all were cats (in keeping with my parents' relentless musical motif, two consecutive orange tabbies had been named for Bach's *Magnificat*—Niffy One and Niffy Two) and were of course aloof and subtle and noninteractive in the ways cats often are. But having a dog was a whole other story. Having a dog was like having a child that was at once fearfully mature (can be left alone for hours at a time) and entirely feebleminded (notably low IQ). And though I had little interest in an actual child of my own, I loved Rex as if he were precisely that. Just three years old, he'd logged thousands of miles in the back of the car and lived at seven different addresses. Throughout this, he never peed indoors, never wandered off, never so much as chewed on a rug. Docile to the extreme and a nonbarker (at twelve weeks old, he'd barked nonstop for an entire day and then given it up entirely), he was a canine Zen master. He was a calming force among all people and even most other dogs. He could lower your blood pressure simply by leaning against your leg. And for these reasons—not to mention the fact that I was the kind of person for whom loving a dog was infinitely easier than loving a human—I had not for one second entertained the thought of not taking him along on my moves.

I had, however, occasionally allowed myself to think about how many more housing options would have been available to me sans pet, especially sans long-haired, slobbering, eighty-five-pound pet. Today as back then, one of the wonders of Los Angeles is that housing, though terrifyingly expensive to buy (somehow, even when the housing market sank into the San Andreas Fault, this remained largely the case), is relatively affordable to rent, at least by the New York City standards to which I still compared just about everything. If you can let go of the idea of living near the beach, you can find a two-bedroom Spanish Colonial–style apartment with arched door-ways, a dishwasher, and off-street parking for about what you might pay for a room in a Brooklyn share. If you have a few dollars to rub together, you can rent yourself a sleek mid-century pad in Santa Monica or a stark industrial loft down-town. But if you have a large dog, it doesn't matter how much money you do or do not have. You need a house with a yard. The yard needs to be fenced. The neighborhood needs to be relatively pedestrian-friendly, since it's nice to be able to walk the dog without butting up against a freeway or a crack house. Moreover, you need a landlord who isn't going to look at an eighty-five-pound yak/dog and tell you he'd rent to a group of unsupervised high-school boys before letting that beast walk on his newly refinished floors. In other words, you have to rent from other dog people. And dog people tend to have dog prop-erties.

Ergo the Beachwood Canyon house. It was, in many respects, a delight: a three-bedroom, three-bath Mediter-ranean villa with Mexican tile and screened French doors and bougainvillea bushes arcing around the iron gates. It was also exploding with debris: dog poop on the patio, dog hair on every piece of furniture, and all manner of dog- and human-related clutter on every possible surface. At night, the border collies ascended and descended the stairs as though they were train-ing for a boxing match. During the day, they flung themselves in and out of the dog door until I had no choice but to close it, which caused them to whine like toddlers. Rex just stood there and stared at them blankly, the canine equivalent to shaking your head in pity.

It was shades of Dani's place all over again. How had I managed to do this to myself once more? Why was I again holding myself hostage in someone else's chaos? Where did I get this uncanny knack for moving to places that, thanks to lack of drawer space or floor space or drinkable water, ultimately proved to be as uninhabitable as they were ostensibly desirable?

As my brother and I used to say (actually, as we still say), duh, duh, and duh. It was all so woefully obvious. When you're more concerned about where your dog goes to the bathroom than where you go to the bathroom, the chances that you'll sign a lease on a decent property go down considerably. I realized this one morning while sitting on the terrace, attempting to eat breakfast al fresco among a flurry of stuffing that one of the border collies had ripped from the sofa. I had a bruise on my leg that I'd incurred by walking into an elliptical trainer I hadn't noticed because it was doubling as a clothes rack. I decided I had to move right away. I would sign a yearlong lease and not break it under any circumstances. I called the friend of the friend and told him I had to leave. He sent for his dogs. Apparently, they loved New York.

I was embarrassed to be moving again, but I felt I was making progress, mostly because the next house might as well have had my name spray painted across the front. It was a farmhouse. Right there in L.A. Granted, it didn't look *exactly* like a farmhouse. If you were actually in the country, you would not point to this house and think, "That's where the farmer and his wife sit down to Rice-A-Roni every night." But against the backdrop of palm trees and steep hills and tattooed young people riding fixed-gear bicycles on the sidewalks, it almost looked as if it had blown in from Nebraska on the winds of a tornado. It was a 1908 Dutch Colonial with yellow clapboard siding and a slate roof, a redbrick chimney, and creaky steps leading to a wide-planked wooden stoop. When I happened to drive by this place and saw a For Rent sign on the fence, I was so afraid of someone snatching it up—never mind that it had been available for weeks—that I called the number on the sign twelve times in less than two hours.

This neighborhood was the aforementioned Silver Lake, an ultra-trendy area east of Hollywood that was still slightly funky in places. Latino families who'd lived there for generations now shared the streets with hipsters who had a fondness for converted bio-diesel Mercedeses and rockabilly hairstyles. Silver Lake is about twenty miles from the beach and in the summer can be twenty degrees warmer and considerably smoggier. But the housing prices are cheaper, and the people tend to be less proselytizing (though this is a generalization about a generalization) about things like soy and the healing powers of "body work" (I'm not talking about cars), and after my less-than-stellar experiences in Topanga and Venice, I'd decided that as much as I loved the ocean breezes I was an east sider at heart.*

When talking to non-Angelenos, I'm often tempted to explain the "east side" by saying that it is to L.A. what Brooklyn now is to New York City or Oakland to the Bay Area or Belltown to Seattle. It's where the cool kids live, or where the gentrifiers do their gentrifying, or where rich but not obscenely rich people can pay $850,000 for a three-bedroom house as opposed to $1.3 million for a condo on the west side. But gentrification issues notwithstanding, the east side of L.A.

---

* I say "east sider" for lack of a better term and with full awareness that, according to many Angelenos, Silver Lake and its adjacent neighborhoods do not technically constitute the east side. To many, the east side and the west side are divided by the L.A. River. This is despite the fact that many west siders (that is, those living west of the 405 freeway in places like Santa Monica) consider anything east of the Beverly Center to be on the east side. They're wrong about that, but it's ultimately too tiresome to get into.

is not Brooklyn or Oakland or Belltown. It is its own region comprised of highly individualized neighborhoods—Los Feliz, Silver Lake, Echo Park, Eagle Rock, Highland Park, Mount Washington—and sections within those neighborhoods—too many to name here—that are themselves their own things. I won't launch into a geographical treatise here (I'd get it wrong anyway; everyone who hasn't lived there thirty years or more gets accused of getting it wrong), but suffice it to say these are the city's old neighborhoods. Hilly and hot and swirling with vegetation and murals and taco trucks and—in many pockets— more brown skin than white, these are the regions where populations of artists and radicals in the 1930s and 1940s morphed into heavily Latino populations in the 1950s and 1960s. In the 1970s, Silver Lake became a locus of gay culture, and Echo Park became a gangland. By the 1990s, Silver Lake was brimming with hipsters, and Echo Park was slowly beginning its rise into a "desirable" neighborhood. In 1995, a six-bedroom Queen Anne Victorian in the Angelino Heights section of Echo Park would have sold for under $100,000. Less than a decade later, its asking price would be $1 million or more. And just to put it in perspective, a few miles away on the west side (where a lot of people have never heard of or would be afraid to come to Echo Park) such a property could cost $6 million.

Anyway, it was now 2003. The rent on the urban farmhouse, which was in the heart of Silver Lake near an adult video store and a Catholic elementary school, was a very urban $2,000 a month. This was definitely on the high end of my price range, but the place had leaded-glass windows and a working fireplace and a built-in floor-to-ceiling china cabinet. There was a small bedroom downstairs and two more rooms upstairs. I'd have room for two of my three beds. Never mind that the kitchen was small and poorly configured with a tiny, ancient stove and no dishwasher. Never mind that you had to park on the street. Never mind that the house's sole bathroom was right off the kitchen, a location that, should nighttime visits be necessary, would require stumbling through four separate rooms and descending a dark staircase. Never mind that if I'd spent another week or two looking at rentals, I could probably have found something better and cheaper, maybe even with a dishwasher and central air-conditioning. Patience wasn't my racket that fall. I needed a house of my own right away.

Part of the reason, I'm embarrassed to say, is that I had a date. This was a very big deal. Lest you thought in my account of the previous few years I've been coyly omitting any mention of romance, I'm afraid that there was nothing to omit. I had an ongoing platonic friendship with Ex, but when it came to real boyfriends or real dates or even just flirty encounters at Trader Joe's (why is it that even the most banal exchange at Trader Joe's—"where's the frozen rice?" for example—sounds as though you're asking if someone's an Aquarius?), my life had been nunlike for nearly two years.

Not that this bothered me significantly. Not that I'd even really much noticed. That's because moving, like chocolate and sunshine, stirs up many of the same chemicals you ostensibly produce when you're in love. At least it does for me. Like a new lover, a new house opens a floodgate of anticipation and trepidation and terrifying expectations fused with dreamy distractions. It's all encompassing and crazy making. You can't concentrate at work. You space out while driving. Granted, you're buying curtains and dish drainers and wastebaskets instead of getting manicures and buying lingerie, but the adrenaline rush is shockingly similar: you close your eyes at night and see only your new kitchen; you meet your friends for lunch and can speak only of your closet space.

No wonder I hadn't needed sex. I was drowning in the eros of real estate. But after five whirlwind romances with various households, the sudden opportunity to revisit the human version of a relationship was surprisingly compelling. (I also worried that I was one holiday season away from turning into one of those people who send Christmas cards with photos of their dogs.)

Hoping to prevent such a fate, I'd allowed a tall, light-haired man whose acquaintance I'd made some weeks earlier to pick me up at the house in Beachwood Canyon and take me to watch Chinese acrobats perform at the Hollywood Bowl. This went well enough—it's hard to have a bad time under the summer night sky in the breezy folds of the Cahuenga Pass—but despite my date's good looks and the romantic nature of the setting I'd found myself hoping he wouldn't so much as hold my hand that night. It would have been all wrong. Not because he was all wrong for me (he was, but that would be revealed later), but because he had absolutely no idea who I was. Since I wasn't living in my own place and, in my mind, couldn't have possibly conveyed anything to him about my true essence, I might as well not have been there at all. It didn't matter that I was wearing my own clothes and speaking my own thoughts and laughing my own laugh. All that mattered was the scene into which he stepped when I opened the door to him. All that mattered was that the furniture and artwork and kitchen supplies and the damn elliptical trainer had not been of my choosing. Two of the three dogs were not mine. The water glass I'd handed him was the product of someone else's shopping trip to IKEA rather than my own. The result was that I felt invisible, unaccounted for, even a little nonexistent. And for those reasons alone (of course, there were others, though they seemed not worth thinking about at the time)

I refused to see the tall, light-haired man again until I'd fully moved into the urban farmhouse in Silver Lake.

Therein ensued the most elaborate set of second-date preparations in history. In the span of two weeks, I not only moved myself in but also had the entire interior of the house painted, purchased and installed thirteen white opaque window shades and/or billowing white curtains, bought a shower curtain from Target and a coffee table and two nightstands from a Moroccan-tile furniture boutique, had a dog door cut into the back door (with begrudging permission from the landlady), had a ceiling fan installed over my bed, and purchased a 1950s nickel-and-glass Czech chandelier and installed it over a late Victorian dining table I'd bought in Nebraska. Given that it was, yet again, autumn in Los Angeles and the temperature was in the nineties and the air was choked with smoke from the burning mountains, I went to Home Depot and bought one of the few window air conditioners left in stock. It must have weighed 150 pounds, yet I dragged it out of the car, up the front steps, into the house, and up the staircase with the superhuman strength with which I'd carried my futon back in college.

Miraculously, I got the air conditioner in the window without dropping it onto the patio below. Miraculously, it cooled the room, even though the house was barely insulated and the autumn sun was almost as merciless as it had been in Topanga Canyon the year before. Armed with a controlled climate, subtle yet distinctive window dressings, and a spectacular paint color scheme (the living room walls were a sharp rococo blue, which was offset by a warm beige in the dining room; the guest room, in a misstep, was a dusty pink), I then began the process of getting ready for a big night out. Which is to say I took a shower and got dressed.

In other words: no manicure, no eyebrow wax, no new pair of shoes or jeans. I didn't know it then, but this was a major turning point in the history of my self-presentation. The appearance of my house had officially become more important than my own appearance. After decades of worrying about my hair and my thighs, I was now mainly concerned about whether a picture was crooked on the wall.

Later, of course, I'd see that part of what was happening was that the tall, light-haired man himself was considerably less interesting than the adult, urban world that a date with him represented. As I'd waited for him to pick me up at the Beachwood Canyon house for the first date, it had occurred to me that the type of date where you were fetched at your door, driven somewhere, and eventually returned home was utterly alien to my life experience. In fact, even the word "date," as archaic and "socially constructed" as my die-hard Vassar sensibilities led me to construe it, seemed charged with the promise of my new California frontier.

That's because until that point I'd lived in the kinds of places where dating took the form of a "meet up" that morphed into "hanging out" and then perhaps "hooking up." I'm not, mercifully, a member of the current twenty- and early-thirty-something generation, which apparently enjoys (or doesn't enjoy) "hooking up" with supposedly platonic friends as a way of avoiding the hassles of dating (in the early 1990s we Generation Xers preferred to hide behind flannel shirts and worry about AIDS). But during my eight-plus years in New York, nobody once showed up at my door and then took me out. In a noncar culture that simply isn't done. You meet in a bar, in a restaurant, on a street corner, or in a subway station. I had not one but two boyfriends in New York who repeatedly insisted on meeting up *on the train itself,* the idea being that if we left our apartments at precisely the right moment and boarded a pre-agreed-upon car of a pre-agreed-upon subway train, we'd be on our way to that grunge show/dive bar/Film Forum screening of *Das Boot* in no time. The stress involved in these maneuvers was not insignificant; they also failed about as often as they worked. Let's recall that this was before anyone really had cell phones, let alone sent SMS messages or Twittered. If you lost someone in this sort of operation, you'd have to call his answering machine from a pay phone and hope that he called from another pay phone and checked his messages. At least the era of my parents' message-retrieving beeper had passed by then.

Maybe dating in New York is different now that the bulk of my demographic lives in Brooklyn, where it's easier to have a car and you can conceivably double-park while you run up to retrieve your paramour from her Cobble Hill brownstone (though I kind of doubt it). But for much of my life as a young single person, a date was a thing you showed up to rather than waited for. Due to roommates and other features of soul-crushingly expensive cities (rats, roaches, bedrooms large enough for only a twin-sized bed), it was possible to have protracted sexual relationships wherein one party never saw the other's living quarters. My last year in New York involved one such relationship and when I finally saw the guy's apartment and noticed that he owned a copy of not only *What Color Is Your Parachute?* but also *The Complete Idiot's Guide to 20th-Century History,* I decided to quit not just the guy (not that I needed too much convincing by then) but New York entirely. When I got to Nebraska, I had approximately one date with Ex (wherein I did not let him come to my house, because he was a complete stranger) before I essentially let him move in. As embarrassing as that is, it also turns out to be the way a lot of people "date" in Lincoln, Nebraska. Which is to say that not even circulating among the car-driving, full-sized-bed-owning echelons guarantees admission to the dating echelons.

But California was grown-up land. I could feel it in so many ways. Unlike the woman-child who'd traipsed through the streets of New York in clunky shoes and Kmart underwear, unlike the would-be iconoclast who struck poses in the Nebraska cornfields while trying fruitlessly to "keep it real," I was now, for once and at last, in concert with my surroundings. And as I waited for the tall, light-haired man to arrive at the Silver Lake house for our second date, a wave of self-love washed over me. After eighteen residences in fifteen years, four of them dorm rooms, three of them crammed with other people's furniture, the others so inappropriate in so many ways, I was finally in my own ample space with my own stuff. After fourteen roommates, one tyrannical building super, one live-in boyfriend, and two dogs that weren't mine, I was finally the queen of my lovingly decorated castle. It was me and my furniture against the world.

Naturally, Mr. Tall, Light-Haired didn't stand a chance. Though I dated him for five months, which was about four months and two weeks longer than I should have (he knew his way around town, and, I'll admit, it's perhaps a bit too easy to keep a boyfriend around just because he knows which way to turn off a freeway exit), I think I can safely say that the highlight of the relationship was the eight or so seconds it took him to walk through my front door for the first time and behold the awesomeness of my taste and self-sufficiency (and he liked the place; he really, really liked it!). In one perfect moment, the house fused my real self and my fantasy version of myself into one glorious—if unmanicured—entity. Here was a woman with azure walls and leaded-glass windows! Here was a woman with no roommates, no shared walls, and an air conditioner! How could anyone not fall for her instantly? How could she not be irresistible to every man, woman, child, and pet who had the occasion to cross her threshold? And how, in turn, could the self-possessing effects of all this experience and all these beautiful objects and all this space not allow her to see the love and irresistibility of others?

I don't know, but I failed to love Tall, Light-Haired nonetheless. Though I spent the ensuing months in a rather exhausting effort to convince myself that our spectacular incompatibility (despite his appealing Midwestern roots, he was a believer in astrology and—troublingly—scented candles) was really a case of my being judgmental (I was, he said, "closed off to the possibility of transformation"), what was really happening was that I was falling in love not with any person but with the idea of living alone in my very own space. When I was with him, I couldn't wait to get home. When he was over, I secretly wanted him to leave.

Instead of being smitten with him, I was smitten with the dynamic between myself and my living quarters. I was in love with the notion of myself as a person who had agency over her physical surroundings, who had taste and the means to use it, who had enough square footage so that everything—even the mateless earrings and broken exercise equipment and not-quite-empty tubes of sunscreen that constitute the grubby detritus of every woman's home—could be tucked away in some rightful, discreet closet or drawer. There was joy in simply inhabiting a room. The act of walking from the kitchen to the front door brought on a kind of reverie. When I was not muddling through dinners or uninspired overnights with my ill-chosen beau, I was reading the newspaper on the weathered wooden stoop with my dog by my side. When I was not having arduous, pointless meetings with Hollywood executives about my various nonideas, I was tracing my finger down the folds of the living room curtains and staring out the window. When I wasn't wiping the kitchen counters or attempting to write something more substantial than an e-mail, I was propping my feet up on the large desk that took up nearly an entire wall of my large office and drinking my second glass of wine while listening to Diana Krall (an upgrade from Suzanne Vega). And while I sometimes thought I wanted a lover so I could share this bliss with someone, the truth was that I just wanted a witness. I wanted someone to see my home, admire it, admire me, and then leave.

Finally, as though I realized I needed to spend more quality time with my house, I broke up with the tall, light-haired man (he was hardly surprised; in fact, I daresay he was relieved). I did this two days after my thirty-fourth birthday. I came very close to doing it *on* my thirty-fourth birthday, to simply getting up and walking out of the restaurant he'd insisted on taking me to even though I'd wanted to go elsewhere (I can't remember the details, though I'm afraid something like "Mars in Capricorn" might have factored into his argument), but I restrained myself out of politeness. I also came close to breaking up with him the next day but did not do so because it was Valentine's Day and I didn't want to be vile.

You'd think by age thirty-four a person would have figured out that there's nothing humane about dumping someone on February 15 rather than on February 14. You'd think that after thirty-four years of having a February 13 birthday, I would have realized that if I'm not particularly enthused about the person I'm dating, it's best to dispatch with him by Martin Luther King Day. You'd think these things, but somehow for me that year any wisdom I'd acquired over time had taken a sabbatical and sent a tenebrous inertia in its place. If I was apathetic about dumping Tall, Light-Haired, I was equally apathetic in other areas, too. In fact, unless it involved home decor, home improvement, or thinking about and looking at other houses, I wasn't much up for it.

Preposterously, I had spent the holiday season and early part of the year consumed with the hypothetical notion of renovating the Silver Lake house (surely walls could be knocked down, the kitchen expanded, a bathroom added). I'd rationalized the fixation by making secret plans to buy the property, even though it wasn't for sale. When the plans became so evolved that I actually called my landlady and asked if she'd entertain an offer, her response—that she wouldn't consider anything less than $1 million—managed to send me into convulsions. I don't remember much about this time in my life, but I do remember crying so hard about my inability to buy the Silver Lake house that my jaw ached the next day. Worse, I woke up to what at the time felt like the saddest scene in the world: a beautiful house that suddenly seems unbeautiful because the person living in it doesn't own it and never will. As though I'd been transported back to the apartment on West 100th Street, which had similarly delighted me until it became clear that I'd never live there without roommates, the Silver Lake house now felt like a way station, the architectural equivalent of a lover you take until you can find someone to actually love. Realizing that my affections for it ran in inverse proportion to my ability to hire a contractor and alter it, I decided it was time to move on. Now, however, the move would be final. I would stop being a house slut. I would stop living in houses and leaving them. I would buy something and stay there. Preferably immediately and preferably forever.

It was, by now, 2004. We were not at the apogee of the market, but we were getting there. The way I've always imagined it is this: if the real estate bubble were a distended piece of chewing gum in the mouth of a teenage girl, it would have been about the size of a lemon at that point—formidable but not out of control. By early 2005 the bubble would have covered her nose and eyes, and by the end of that year it would have been as big as her head. By 2007 it would have deflated slightly, and by 2008 it would have popped and been all over her face. By 2009 she'd have choked and died on the gum, but let's not go there now.

Instead, let's remember 2004. Money was everywhere: talk of it, displays of it, envy of those who had it, and pity for those who didn't. In the spring of 2004, you could find a thirty-year fixed interest rate of 5 percent. Adjustable-rate loans were, of course, practically falling off trucks—not just shiny, new expensive trucks but old, beat-up trucks, garbage trucks, even. People were paying $600,000 or $700,000 for properties that, four years earlier, would have been worth $200,000. People were taking out low-interest loans for $700,000, buying houses for $550,000, and using the difference to buy Range Rovers and vacations in Anguilla.

As high as the housing prices were, everyone knew they were only going to get higher. People who already owned knew their asset values were only going up, and people who didn't own but wanted to knew their chances of getting into the market were only going down. Terrified of getting left behind, first-time buyers grabbed on to those prices as though clinging to an aircraft carrying refugees out of the jungle. For my part, I was sure that if I didn't get in quickly, I wouldn't get in at all. In Los Angeles, dilapidated hovels in sketchy neighborhoods were garnering multiple offers within hours of being listed.

Adjustable mortgages and record-low interest rates aside, "middle class" houses (those with three bedrooms) were now available only to the rich. Moreover, as though the nation's major religions had coalesced into a single doctrine and formed a cult of real estate, no one seemed able or willing to speak of any other subject. If there were major news events going on, I cannot recall them now. If there was anyone from any walk of life who did not appear to have some kind of stake in this gamble, I didn't know the person. My hairdresser, various yoga teachers, and of course my dental hygienist: they all seemed engaged in a constant stream of chatter about granite countertops or closing costs, loans or reverse mortgages or termite inspections.

Because of all this—and also because perhaps no one on earth was as predisposed to joining in on this craziness as I was—I developed a brainsickness that would last well into the following year. It's difficult to talk about this phase without sounding hyperbolic, but the alternative—dullness born of lethargy—is worse. I know this because I had two speeds at the time: urgency and apathy. That is to say, I was either thinking and talking in such exaggerations that I didn't seem quite sane ("I will literally *die* if I don't find a house by June"; "that Craftsman went for $200,000 over the asking price, it's an *apocalypse!*") or sprawled out on the couch unable to face anything that didn't involve searching the Multiple Listing Service.

And then there were the TV shows. *Trading Spaces, Design on a Dime, House Hunters,* and Debbie Travis's *Facelift.* In the wake of the boom, the Home & Garden TV cable channel, which actually started back in 1994, had exploded in popularity, offering a round-the-clock infusion of house porn for wretches like me. I watched, of course. Like just about anyone with a pulse (any woman with a pulse), I couldn't get enough HGTV (and the competing shelter smut on Bravo and Life-time and TLC) in 2004. I watched, even though it ultimately left me cold. Actually, it left me worse than cold. It made me feel emotionally bloated, as though I'd gorged myself on Styro-foam, as though I'd tried to eat insulation.

That's because many of the houses looked as if they were made of Styrofoam. With rare exceptions, the programs struck me as guided tours of ordinariness, fonts of mediocre ideas disguised as "eclecticism." Occasionally, something would strike my fancy—a casbah-inspired pergola on a Brooklyn deck, a genuinely innovative window treatment, an episode of the international edition of *House Hunters* featuring a British couple shopping for an old country manor—but for the most part the whole enterprise felt hollow, desensitizing, like literal porn. It depressed me to think about how many Realtors and contractors and decorators and even carpenters—people whose professions once existed outside the realm of media—now felt compelled to try to make it in show business. It depressed me even more that regular people would sacrifice their privacy, their dignity, and often the (entirely decent) orig-inal floor plans of their houses in the hopes that their mar-riages would be saved or their lives elevated by a bossy, telegenic decorator. The fact that I watched it all anyway, the fact that innocent channel surfing often resulted in three hours lost to the blandishments of wall stencils and beaded throw pillows, only added to the dueling forces of my house obsession and my growing self-disgust with that obsession. If only I'd known it was just the beginning of both.

Within twenty-four hours of being told the Silver Lake house wasn't for sale, I'd called a Realtor and asked him to show me what was. The Realtor, a former stand-up comedian named Michael who'd come highly recommended by a Vassar friend, informed me that I was "right on the edge of getting priced out of the market." What that meant was that most small, two-bedroom "starter homes" in the area were going for around $500,000. I could afford up to about $400,000. If I was going to get in on the action, Michael told me as he zipped me around my desired neighborhoods in his convertible Audi TT, I needed to act fast.

For the record, Michael was not a pushy guy. Despite the fervor of the moment, no one was pressuring me to do anything, except maybe subconsciously my mother, whose hardwired real estate obsession was finding new life in my own (from three thousand miles away, she e-mailed me listings for "affordable" places in neighborhoods she didn't realize probably had more guns than mailboxes). The mortgage broker I'd retained didn't steer me toward a "creative financing plan," nor did anyone try to get me to consider any house I didn't like. For one thing, they didn't have to; for every house for sale, there were hundreds of potential buyers. For another, I suspect there was something about my quest that was slightly perplexing and therefore vulnerable to not being taken entirely seriously.

Sure, I wasn't the only unmarried woman in the market for a house (single women were and still are the nation's second-largest group of first-time home buyers after married couples). I wasn't even the only single woman in a so-called creative profession who aspired to property ownership. But in a city where the majority of "creative" people who can afford a house have made their money writing or directing or acting in television shows about psychic police detectives or movies where the romantic leads fall in love during a montage sequence featuring paddleboats and miniature golf, saying, "I'm a freelance print journalist and I'd like a loan for $350,000" is a little bit questionable. It was not lost on me that at the time I began working with a Realtor, my professional projects consisted of a low-paying magazine essay and a novel on which I'd been on page 50 for five months. When my mortgage broker asked if I had any steady paying work on the horizon, I proudly told him I'd accepted a one-semester guest professorship at an art college in the fall for $2,200. When he asked me what kind of "loan product" for what kind of property I wanted, I said all I was asking for was a plain and simple thirty-year fixed loan and a nice, nondecrepit house in an unhorrendous neighborhood for $400,000 or less.

Apparently, I was asking way too much. For all of Michael's supposed comic talents (he had, he told me, actually made money as a stand-up), there was really nothing humorous about our excursions. Though he did his best to lighten the mood—"you could stage a production of *Noises Off* in here," he said of a begrimed shack that had about six more doors than it should have—the quality of the inventory in my price range was so lacking that levity seemed as out of reach as a decent house. Michael took me to see broken bungalows that were sliding down hills, ranch houses whose kitchens and bathrooms must have been designed by children, and at least one place that suggested Ted Kaczynski had kept a second home near a needle-strewn underpass of the Hollywood Freeway. We looked at houses that would have required me to pay $3,000—an amount that was both annoyingly large and criminally small—to relocate the large Latino families living inside them, which was, for me, a deal breaker. In many cases, when I say "looked," I mean "drove by," since, at the time, if a property was occupied by renters, you could not actually go inside until you'd made an offer and had it accepted (in other words, filled out the paperwork and handed over earnest money in the $30,000 range). We were occasionally able to get around this by peeking in the windows or just pushing a decaying door open, like cops on one of those TV dramas created by people who could afford better houses. Often there were no tenants at all, merely doleful evidence of their prior existence—dirty plastic kids' toys, empty one-liter Pepsi bottles, tubs of Spackle pried open and then abandoned as though the house had looked in the face of whoever thought he could patch up the holes and just laughed.

"This is starting to make me lose my will to live," I said to Michael one afternoon as we climbed (he in his Italian shoes, me in my flip-flops) over a chicken-wire fence in an "up and coming" neighborhood.

"I'm just respecting your price point," he said. "If you want, we can see some properties that represent more of a stretch for you, but I don't want you to end up disappointed."

This is the classic Realtor trick, of course. At least in a brisk market. They show you crappy stuff that makes you want to blow your brains out, and then, after you've lowered your standards to roughly the level of the earth's crust, they start ratcheting you back up again. In fairness to Michael, whom I'd grown fond of despite the guided tours of hell he called house hunting, I'm sure he was, indeed, respecting my price point. But I don't think he was surprised when, after touring an open house whose listing agent was legally required to hand out flyers explaining that there was a psychiatric hospital *less than two hundred feet away*—"maybe you could just live *in* the hospital," Michael suggested—I clenched my jaw and said, "Okay, maybe I can go up to $420,000."

The week we started looking at nicer properties also happened to be a week that my mother came to visit. Naturally, she was elated by our schedule of activities. She'd visited me a handful of times over the course of my various moves, but she'd never had so much fun as now. Clearly, she'd missed her calling as a Realtor, maybe even as a used-car salesman. While touring open houses on a Sunday afternoon, she didn't hesitate to make decorating and furniture layout suggestions for houses that were $100,000 or $200,000 more than I could afford. "Oh Meghan, this is your house!" she exclaimed as we entered a pristinely restored three-bedroom Craftsman in the neighborhood that had become my first choice, the hills of Echo Park, which lay just east of Silver Lake. "You could put your desk right here! And look at this yard! Rex will love it!" The house was listed at $627,000. It eventually sold for $779,000.

Other houses my mother declared perfect for me were a hillside contemporary for $889,000, another Craftsman with a smaller yard but a built-in breakfast table and benches for $603,999, and a Victorian bungalow with a picket fence and restored woodwork and wainscoting in the kitchen for $527,000. The Victorian really got to me, so much so that I still think about it today. It was a unique, adorable house—not unlike the Silver Lake place, though more logically laid out— in a not altogether safe neighborhood. Low-rent apartment buildings interspersed themselves between small wooden clapboard or Spanish stucco houses, some well kept, some not. The area was a known crime zone, and although you'd think that would have been enough to put me off, the house struck me as a big valentine made of wood and slate and glass. If I closed my eyes, it seemed literally heart shaped. I wanted to hug it.

It needed work. Of course it did; could I have loved it otherwise? The plumbing, evidently, was iffy, and the garage appeared rather corroded. There was no backyard, and the tract of grass inside the picket fence was far too close to the street to represent any kind of sanctuary. Still, I stewed over the place for a week (an eternity in that market), weighing the wainscoting against the plumbing, the restored woodwork against the bad garage, the stained-glass window in the second-floor garret versus the fact that, according to a lengthy article in the alternative weekly newspaper, local hoodlums had been responsible for several drive-by shootings and a car bomb last year. I then remembered that the place was $527,000 and therefore $107,000 beyond my budget. When I broke the news to my mother, the car bomb detail softened the blow considerably.

"When you find the right house you'll know it," she said.

She was right. I did always know when I found the right house, but thanks to my new practice of shopping above my means, I could never afford it. I found a two-bedroom Mediterranean with a detached office that was right for me, a storybook cottage in the hills above Silver Lake Reservoir that was right for me, and, most shatteringly, a rustic, bohemian Craftsman–cum–hunter's cabin with skylights, sleeping lofts, and a pool that, with about $300,000 worth of foundation work, would have been more right for me than my very own skin. Unfortunately, all of these properties turned out to be right for people with about twice as much money to spend as I had.

True scholarship requires obsession, baseless fixation, an absorption with the kinds of minutiae that, to the average person, holds about as much interest as varieties of chimney soot. Given the consumerist, manic, solipsistic nature of this pursuit, there are of course countless Internet enablers to choose from. Not just Craigslist, but also realtor.com, MLS.com, ziprealty.com, redfin.com, and my own imaginary start-up icantevengetup togotothebathroombecausethenexthousemightbeit.com. I looked at realtor.com so frequently it appeared on my computer browser if I so much as typed the letter *r*, my old stand-bys like radiodiaries.com and rollingstone.com fading into the background like a pet forgotten because of a new baby. Quickly exhausting the listings in my immediate vicinity, I eventually became expert on home values elsewhere, taking a curious solace in my discovery that a three-bedroom, two-bathroom Craftsman back in Lincoln was merely $110,000 and, even though I have no connection to the place, a similar house in Portland, Oregon, could be had for $340,000. Maybe I liked knowing that should the Southern California housing market ultimately elude me, I could always go someplace where prices were on a human scale. Maybe I also liked the reminder that as "basic" a right of passage as buying a home was supposed to be, some regions were more basic than others. In most moments, I knew it wasn't just a house I was after but, rather, proof of my existence. The house was not just a house but also an I.D. badge for adulthood, for *personhood* even. It was the only thing that would make me desirable, credible, even human.

I was quite a treat to be around during this period. Not only was I unable to carry on a conversation about anything other than brokers' fees and pocket listings, but I had inadvertently entered something of a second latency period. This is not to be confused with my mini-latency period of a few years earlier, when I'd literally been moving around too much to think about dating. This time, I had opportunities to date but no interest in taking advantage of them. I didn't even want to have sex. The reasons for this were probably manifold and best left to a psychiatrist, but as far as I was concerned, I was saving myself for home ownership. I mean that quite literally. I did not want to get into a relationship or even go on a date until I owned property. I did not want a man crossing my threshold, drinking my tap water, or even parking at my curb until that threshold, tap water, and curb were in some way legally registered in my name. I did not even want to meet a potential romantic partner until I could look him in the eye from my bar stool and say, without apology or drama, "I own a house."

In honor of this vow of delayed gratification, I kept myself looking and feeling about as sexy as your average meter maid. My hair, though always short, was entirely too short and, thanks to a misguided effort to come across as "feisty," an unfortunate shade of red (make that shades, since the red had a way of quickly turning pinkish and then orange). There was a bloated, phlegmatic quality to my physical being. I was doughy and epicene and also strangely hyper. Anyone who encountered me during this period found himself face-to-face with a sort of asexual monomaniac. Though I could stumble through polite, non-housing-related conversation for twenty to thirty minutes, any opportunity I sensed to change the subject to down payments and appraisal fees would be seized like the second-to-last piece of shrimp on a cocktail platter. To anyone who would listen, I nattered on about the houses for sale that I hated, the houses not for sale that I coveted, the envy aroused by those who bought ten years earlier during the slump, the smugness of sellers, the desperation of buyers, the calamity of it all.

This is embarrassing but not exactly mortifying. Mostly because everyone was talking like this at the time. My conversation may have been tiresome, but it was hardly aberrant. At parties, cliques would form in corners around topics like these—comprised mostly of women but including plenty of men, too—and the discussion would become so animated and loud that eventually the hostess would come over and say, "What's going on here?" only to find herself helplessly drawn in. A woman I'd befriended the previous year, a writer named Carina, happened also to be house hunting during this time, and the two of us soon found ourselves bonded together as if real estate obsession secreted some kind of hallucination-inducing superglue. Like pregnant women who share and dissect every aspect of gestation with painstaking detail and outsized enthusiasm, we spent hours visiting open houses and driving around strange neighborhoods one of us (usually me) was convinced was the next hot place. We spent several times that many hours talking to each other on the phone about Carina's latest conversation about mortgages with her financial whiz brother or my latest theory about why buying a house that came with a rental unit and therefore required me to be a landlord "might actually make me a better writer" (this theory totally escapes me now and, mercifully, was never tested).

If there's any one experience that encapsulates the inflated home values and near surrealism of that time period, it was the afternoon Carina and I went to an open house in the neighborhood of Mount Washington. Neither of us, her especially, particularly wanted to live in Mount Washington, but it had a reputation for slightly lower-priced houses than much of what was available in Silver Lake and Echo Park, and I'd suggested we give the neighborhood a gander. After failing to find the first two houses on our list because the streets depicted on my MapQuest printout appeared to have no relationship to the actual streets of Mount Washington, we found the third property, a small, cabinlike house on a wooded hillside.

Between the used-car-lot-style flags and the "Another fine

property from Blah Blah realty" sign in the yard, a line of about a dozen people had formed by the doorway. Despite the shabbiness of the house—the paint was chipped, and the roof appeared to be sliding off like a loose toupee—I took that as a sign that the place was so much in demand that it simply could not contain all the people who wanted to look at it. This turned out to be true, although not in a good way. In fact, it was true in the most depressing way possible, which is to say that only six people were allowed inside at once because the foundation wasn't guaranteed to hold any more than that. Notices posted on the front door and on the walls stated disclosures about electricity (there was none in the kitchen and study), plumbing (apparently there were sewage "issues"), and rodents (rats and mice definitely; opossums maybe).

A large deck of at least two hundred square feet, which may have been larger than the living room, jutted out from the hillside, offering a sweeping view of pine trees and palm trees and the distant decks of neighbors. It was easily the best thing about the house. Unfortunately, it was barricaded with caution tape because, as the agent explained, it was "unsafe for walking on." It would, in fact, need to be torn down. And while she was on the subject, the agent said (and not at all sheepishly, which should have been astonishing but was commonplace in 2004) the deck wasn't the only thing that needed to be torn down. Given the condition of the roof, the foundation, and the walls, potential buyers were to take it under advisement that the entire house should probably be torn down. If we had any questions, she said, we could talk to the owners, who, contrary to custom, were actually on the premises. She then gestured to a stained orange couch on which three elderly people of questionable hygiene were staring into space smoking cigarettes, their ashes cascading around a glazed ceramic ashtray on the floor, sometimes landing in it, sometimes not.

The asking price on this house was $425,000. I'm pretty sure it ultimately sold in the mid-$500,000 range.

When Carina and I went back to the car (I remember that we were wedged between a new BMW and an Audi; people who drove cars like that were looking at houses like this), one of us said she felt like throwing up, and the other said she felt like crying. I can't remember which of us said what, but I do remember that this trip was the beginning of the end of our house-hunting phase. We were no longer excited pregnant ladies as much as we were mutual enablers of a mounting addiction.

"I can't do this anymore," Carina said to me as I made the first of several wrong turns on the way home. "There's something very, very wrong in all of this."

"I know," I said. "If only I'd been ready to buy a few years ago. Why do I come so late to everything? Why do I miss the boat every time?"

"Because we're Gen X," she said. "We were born both too late and too early. The economic forces conspired against us, and now we're fucked and the boomers live in mansions they bought for $67 back in the early 1980s and we're destined to live our lives paying rent to guys who wear tinted eyeglasses and Members Only jackets."

She didn't say exactly that, but she came close and might as well have. It's one of the reasons we'd hit it off before our entire friendship got strung out on real estate. She quit looking for a house shortly after that. She was in a relationship that was at that awkward, one-year point at which thinking about the future feels both necessary and premature. Though she was willing to buy a house by herself, part of her was shopping not just for *her* house but for something that could potentially accommodate another person, a place for a couple and maybe even a family. That's why when she saw the house on Escalada Terrace, a short, breathtakingly steep Echo Park street lined with bougainvillea and oversized, flowering succulents, she called me from the car.

"I just saw a supercute place," she said. "It's too small for me, but you might like it. It's $475,000, but it's been on the market for like a month, so maybe they'd go down."

"There has to be something wrong with it," I said.

"There's something weird going on with the garage in back," Carina said. "But who cares about that? It has awesome views from the kitchen. And fruit trees."

Fruit trees, I thought. Awesome views. Possibly less than $475,000. By now it was the beginning of June. Summer was sliding into view like one of those expensive cars rolling off an assembly line. I was convinced I was approximately seventeen minutes from being priced out of the market.

Reader, I bought it.

FIVE

I remember next to nothing about the first time I walked into the house on Escalada Terrace. I recall that I liked the street, a steep, sidewalkless road of only a dozen houses or so that dead-ended at the mouth of a voluptuous ten-acre hill. I recall that the front yard was attractively landscaped with cactus trees and blooming bougainvillea. As for the house itself, it was a stucco box, a stout, unremarkable Spanish-style bungalow, built in 1928, with an arch-shaped front door and a flat roof lined with red clay tiles. There were two bedrooms, though one was so tiny it seemed unlikely to fit anything larger than a twin bed. The entire place was about nine hundred square feet, considerably smaller than the Silver Lake house. The majority of those nine hundred square feet was covered with dirty white carpet. Unoccupied for at least the last few months, the place was devoid of furniture. This made the carpet—and the discolored indentations where furniture had once rested on it—an unfortunate main attraction.

Still, my chief reaction to the place was that I didn't hate it. Yes, there was carpet, which was anathema to all members of the Daum family, but I was assured there was wood underneath. This was not my dream house; that was for sure. It was not the Craftsman I longed for or, better yet, a small, shabby Victorian like the one my mother coveted for me in car bomb land. Nothing about it made me tingle, and in no way did I feel as if I'd die if I didn't get it. But it had one very big thing going in its favor: it had been sitting on the market for thirty days.

What that meant was that I was able to make an offer of $432,000 and to eventually accept the seller's counteroffer of $450,000. Because it was 2004 and because Michael prided himself on being a "buyer's agent," meaning he had a whole bag of tricks for making an offer seem as attractive as possible (case in point, his belief that nonround numbers like $432,000 made it seem like you were "serious"), I was encouraged to write a personal letter to the seller imploring him to accept my offer. My letter, which I wrote in barely legible handwriting on one of a box full of Van Gogh water lilies note cards that Michael kept in his desk for such purposes, went like this:

Dear Seller,

I absolutely love your house and I hope very, very, very much that you will seriously consider my offer. As soon as I stepped through the front door I knew it was the place for me. I just know that if I'm lucky enough to live there my dog and I will be happy forever.

Sincerely,

Meghan Daum

I then wrote a check for $13,500 in earnest money, which represented 3 percent of the purchase price. We weren't in Nebraska anymore. I realize that some readers, despite all the housing prices I've heretofore mentioned in these pages, might see such a figure and either (a) shoot oatmeal through their noses or (b) lose all sympathy for a narrator (a single, semi-unemployed one at that) who could or would pay such a sum. But please understand that in Los Angeles then, any property with four walls and a roof that cost under half a million dollars was considered a steal. Never mind that the house on Escalada Terrace was smaller than a lot of Midwestern garages. Never mind that the garage, about which Carina had only been able to say "there's something weird going on," bore a close resemblance to the ruins of Pompeii. During this period in real estate history, house hunting was akin to a form of speed dating in which you have three minutes to decide whether or not you want to marry someone. And even though my house didn't necessarily make me swoon, it didn't make me gag either. So, like a girl who cares more about being married than about whom she's married to, I swallowed my pride and signed the first set of papers.

Then I left town. For nearly the entire escrow period of my home purchase, I was on tour for the paperback edition of the novel about the girl who moves to a fictional Midwestern town (what was left of the advance for which was now being poured into the down payment). In a way, this was a good thing. As I had learned the previous year during the hardcover tour, traveling around the country promoting your book is kind of like having sex with a celebrity. You spend much of your life thinking it must be among the greatest experiences you can have, only to find, if you actually do it (and I'm not saying I have), that it's no different from sex with a nonfamous person and, moreover, has no bearing on the metric of your own fame or lack thereof. In other words, as a person who had dreamed of going on a book tour ever since I'd heard the term (most likely while holed up in one of my many Vassar residences reading *Vanity Fair*—the magazine, not the novel), I had, a year earlier—and predictably—been humbled to learn firsthand just how humiliating the experience can be.

And it was again this year, at least after the first stop, which was just downright strange. The first stop was Austin. Weeks earlier, I'd been offered a magazine assignment that involved going back to a childhood home and seeing how much it had or hadn't changed. Given my obsession with all things with a roof and four walls, this was a no-brainer. Since I was going to be in Austin for the book tour anyway, arrangements were made for me to visit the yellow brick bungalow. And since this trip also happened to correspond to my mother's sixty-second birthday, she decided to fly down and join me. We hadn't visited since 1985, when I'd been in ninth grade. When I walked out to the curb at Austin-Bergstrom International Airport, the air was so humid it felt nearly liquid. My mother, driven by one of her old friends from the days of marching on the capitol steps in support of the ERA, picked me up in a shiny SUV.

"I'm in escrow!" I told her. I'd been waiting to tell her in person, and I said it in the same tone another kind of daughter might have said "I'm engaged" or "I'm pregnant."

"Oh, really?" my mother said. Suddenly she seemed worried, as though the reality were less exciting than the concept. Why did this surprise me? The reality was frightening. It was shopping she loved.

Her friend, on the other hand, couldn't get enough. She'd once been a hippie, but she worked in real estate now.

Austin embraced us like some sort of many-armed creature. Hot as ever and draped in the wisteria and honeysuckle vines I remembered from my youth, the city felt both larger and smaller than I remembered it. The skyline, with the ziggurat of

One Congress Plaza and shiny office buildings and condos along the Colorado River, had been jacked up since we'd last been there, but the streets of my old neighborhood, thick with bamboo shoots and pecan trees, seemed narrower. The surrogate grandparents who'd encouraged us to move to Ridgewood were lost to us now—the man had died some years earlier; the woman was buried under years of Alzheimer's—but their kids, now middle-aged with kids of their own, took us back as though we'd never left. My mother had kept in touch with them intermittently over the years, but even so, the ease with which they slid us into their days astounded me. We celebrated my mother's birthday in a Mexican restaurant, a garrulous party of ten or so shouting across the table and telling the kinds of rambling, homespun stories—tales of do-it-yourself car repairs gone awry and bats caught in attic eaves—that my mother had spent the last twenty-five years being visibly unamused by. Not that she was amused now, but I could tell she was having a good time, or at least some kind of time. I couldn't be sure, of course, but maybe she was even feeling what I was feeling. Maybe she was seeing the wind blow through the cedar trees outside the Mexican restaurant and thinking about how things might have gone differently if she hadn't held her rigid definitions of ambition so dear. Maybe she was beholding this table of mirthful, mortal, ordinary souls and wondering why our family had so rarely found itself at tables like this. Or maybe she wasn't thinking anything. I couldn't presume to know. And I couldn't bring myself to ask.

I did a reading at a bookstore. The mother of one of my old playmates had heard about my appearance and showed up with her daughters—both married, one pregnant—and a handful of others from the neighborhood.

"We know you moved away a long time ago, but we're still claiming you as one of ours," she said.

This seemed like a stretch, but it nearly choked me up anyway.

The next day, my mother and I went to visit the yellow brick bungalow, which was owned by a bachelor herpetologist who'd bought it several years earlier. Filing cabinets lined the rooms, and photographs of frogs and salamanders covered the walls. In the kitchen, the tile my mother had laid down in 1977— shiny red squares designed to look like bricks—was still on the floor, though the brick shapes had worn away almost completely.

And then we saw the mural. It was still there, faded but unmistakable—the chocolate brown circles and squares still floating in a sea of beige, the yellow globules washed out from years of sunlight yet soiled with kitchen grease.

"Oh my God," my mother said. "It's still there."

"You did that?" said the herpetologist. "I always wondered."

"No one painted over it," my mother said. "That's incredible."

"Well, I wasn't going to," the herpetologist said. "It was just too weird."

The rest of the book tour was dominated less by my efforts to sell my book than—for real this time—to buy a house. This was actually a healthy combination of activities in that I was too busy thinking about the house to notice just how few people were buying my book but also too distracted with the book to truly understand what I was getting into with the house. To this day, I believe that if I'd been around during the inspection period, there is a good chance I would have backed out. As it was, I was often thousands of miles away, ordering cheeseburgers from room service and errantly reading faxed inspection reports that I often couldn't make sense of due to bad transmissions, sheer fatigue, or plain inertia. In all cases, I signed them anyway and faxed them back.

As a result of this tele-escrowing, most of the information I received about the house on Escalada Terrace—its precarious retaining walls, its unconventional wiring, the plumbing that dated back to the Coolidge administration, the total disrepair of the garage—was delivered to me on my cell phone by Michael, usually while I was in an airport, walking through a hotel lobby, or riding a shuttle van to or from one of these places. To the seller, I must have been the perfect buyer, a semiconscious first-timer who not only wanted the property but also was desperate just to get home, to *any* home. Within a few weeks, news such as "the garage is uninsurable" sounded like a minor inconvenience compared with the thought of another night at the Sheraton.

Of course, I had a home. I was not a vagrant by any means. The rented house in Silver Lake, with the paint job I'd commissioned not even a year earlier, would have been perfectly fine—and quite a bit larger—to come home to. But it's the temptation of so many suburban-raised children to invent tales of adversity, to create hardscrabble mythologies out of life histories marked by little more than field hockey games and orthodontist appointments. I think of a man I'd once known in New York who lost his student housing and dramatically (in an effort to freeload off various comely women) proclaimed himself "homeless." I think of my own low-rent posturing during those years in New York when I should have been at college: the late nights walking the crumbling streets of Alphabet City, the time I watched a knife fight outside the window of the studio in Greenwich Village, the time I got an HIV test at a

Department of Health free clinic in order to prove some kind of point to myself (other than that I didn't have HIV, which I already knew). I think of some of the perverse rural working-class fantasies I acted out in Nebraska—cooking from cans, fretting over the cost of a house call from a large-animal veterinarian, opening the back door and hollering "dinner's ready" to a guy working under the hood of a pickup with very large tires—and I know that despite physically being in Nebraska in those moments, I was really back in Ridgewood or at Vassar trying to prove to myself I was anything but a person from Ridgewood or Vassar. It was as if all the moving around were less about finding a place to live than about covering the perceived blankness of wherever I was actually "from" with the more colorful wallpaper of wherever I wished I was from.

And so it went with the house on Escalada Terrace. Not only had it taken on the imaginative qualities of a potentially adoptable orphan from a developing country (in other words, not only did I need it; it needed *me*), but I actually found that I almost delighted in hearing about its flaws. Every ominous inspection report elicited half-guilty/half-exhilarating fantasies of rescue. Every bit of bad or weird or inconclusive news ("they're not sure where the property lines are," "the retaining wall is as secure as an anthill," "it seems there was a small electrical fire in 2003") only increased my longing to save it from its ugly-wallpapered, shag-carpeted, fire-hazardous self.

Now that I look back on it, I was also being kind of macho. In the same way that I believed having a house rather than a condo would announce to the world that I was not your average scented-candle-burning, oversized-furniture-owning, husband-seeking single woman (in other words, not Dani) but, rather, someone with a small TV and a big dog who was in absolutely no need of rescue, I believed buying a falling-apart house was sexier than buying a turnkey one. No ordinary house for me! An intrepid, sporting girl such as myself demanded (which is to say "could handle") someplace rustic, maybe even someplace on the verge of decay. Such an obvious defiance of convention, I believed, would ensure that I was downright fabulous. The more my house resembled a cabin, a desert adobe, or an abandoned factory stuck in the middle of a landfill, the more desirable and therefore the less lonely I'd be. "Holy shit, look at her!" the world would say. "She's no Ally McBeal in a twee Boston apartment with her roommate and hallucinations of maternal longing; she's Jennifer Beals living alone with her pit bull in her loft in *Flashdance*. She's not Mary Richards sleeping on a fold-out sofa in an attic apartment; she's Major Houlihan with her own tent in the MASH unit and more balls than all the doctors combined. She may not have a farm, but she's still got a little Willa Cather in her. Someone buy this woman a drink! Make it a double; she can take it! By the way, did we mention she's hot?"

And even though the house, though not by any means in perfect condition, was entirely inhabitable, I told myself—and anyone else who would listen—that the place was a wreck. The small electrical fire, the uninsurable garage, the shaky retaining wall: I upgraded them to full-scale emergencies. I told the folks in Austin that the house I was buying was a "major fixer." I told an entire bookstore audience in Milwaukee that "my next project is not literary but rather a study in retaining-wall repair." I told the guy sitting next to me on the flight back to L.A. that coyotes were currently living in the backyard.

"You're buying this house all by yourself?" most people

asked me. The question delighted me; their shock delighted me; the phony cavalierism of my answer delighted me despite my knowing full well how phony it was.

"Of course," I said. "It's about time my dog and I settle down."

So there I was in the escrow office, signing my name on about three hundred pieces of paper. About half the time the printed name next to the signature line was, simply, "Meghan Daum." The other half of the time it was "Meghan Daum, an unmarried woman." I can only assume this terminology arose out of the Fair Housing Act of 1968, which made it illegal for home sellers and lenders to discriminate based on gender. Before that, any woman signing escrow papers was presumed to be doing so with her husband. Even then, several real estate brokers have told me, she often had to get a "pill letter" from her doctor verifying that she was on birth control and therefore wouldn't get pregnant, quit her job, and lose the income on which the granting of the loan was based.

Recognizing my good fortune in not having to provide a letter saying I hadn't had sex in several months and wasn't planning to until the house was refurbished and decorated to my exact specifications, which might take years, I signed the documents. It took about forty-five minutes. I remember that it was very hot outside—it was July 8, a Thursday, 3:00 p.m.—and the air conditioner was on full blast in the office and the perspiration I'd brought in from the street was now beading on my arms and forehead. My hand was shaking, and I can still see the pictures on the escrow officer's desk: wedding portraits and birthday party photos and a gauzy silhouette from a little girl's first Communion. I remember signing the first document and turning to my left as though there were someone sitting next to me, which of course there wasn't (the seller lived out of town and had signed his paperwork elsewhere; meanwhile, I'd somehow assumed throughout the whole process that Michael would be there for the closing, but of course there was no need for that). For a moment I wondered if I was dreaming the whole event. I'd just made the biggest commitment of my life in the presence of no one but a woman named Irene Diaz. (Was that her name exactly? I can no longer remember, though I'm pretty sure I could recognize those desk photos even today.) I'd just signed away more money and, for all intents and purposes, taken the solemnest vow I'd ever uttered, with a complete stranger as my sole witness.

I needed a companion immediately. I needed the kind of companion to whom you can talk nonsensically, repeat yourself ad nauseam, list the reasons you might have just made a huge mistake, and receive back a corresponding list of reasons that you did the right thing. Alison would have qualified, but she lived on the west side and rarely made the trip east without at least a week's notice. Carina was out of town. No one else sprang immediately to mind. Taking the new house keys in my sweating palm, I jumped in the car, swung by the Silver Lake house, and grabbed the portable stereo from the counter (I'd been assured the electricity in the new place was still on) and a bottle of wine from the fridge, a glass, and a corkscrew (always thinking ahead). I put Rex in the car and drove to the house on Escalada Terrace. If I couldn't be in a dim lounge eating tapas and clinking glasses with a reassuring friend, the very least I could do was go to the house and just sit there, taking it in, receiving the vibrations of my momentous, possibly idiotic decision. If I couldn't drink to it, at least I'd drink in it.

The Sold sign, hanging from a wooden post jammed into the ground like a stern teacher's note ("see me," "let's discuss," "needs improvement"), was the only hint of life on the property. Blank and forlorn from months of nonoccupancy, its window box bereft of flowers, its mail slot jammed with dozens of flyers, in English and in Spanish, advertising lawn care service or pizza delivery or salvation through the teachings of Jehovah's Witnesses, the house was an anemic body crying out for nourishment, a withered plant for whom even a single drop of water might make all the difference. Once I was inside, the carpet hit me like a wave. Without taking a step farther into the house, I tore off a corner and began pulling it up. I did this as if my life depended upon finding an intact wood floor underneath. I didn't care what kind of condition the wood was in, just that it was there and that you could walk on it without falling into the extremely scary crawl space beneath the house. I did this until I'd ripped such a large swath from the tacks—the wood was decent, if splintered and scarred—that the carpet was bunched up in the center of the room like jeans thrown on the floor. Deeming it too heavy to move, I opened the wine—it was now 7:00 p.m., an acceptable cocktail hour—poured it into the glass, plugged the stereo in, and called Rex to come sit on the pile of carpet with me. Having forgotten to bring a CD, I realized that the stereo still had a Cat Stevens's *Greatest Hits* cassette in the tape deck, which had probably been in there since Vassar days. The song that came on, naturally, was "Wild World," official anthem of all striking-out-on-their-own girls everywhere. By the time it got to "Hard Headed Woman," I was already on my third glass of wine and weepily singing along to the lyrics—"and if I find my hard headed woman, I know the rest of my life will be blessed, yes yes yes"—while burying my face in Rex's fur.

In other words, I had arrived! Whereas other single thirty-four-year-old females were getting drunk and crying in rental apartments with the requisite wicker furniture, Moroccan-style throw pillows, and pear-scented candles from Pier 1 Imports, I had the dignity, privilege, and, let's face it, *cojones* to do so in my *own house*. Moreover, once moved in, I would have not wicker furniture but actual antiques. I would have not scented candles but regular candles that went in pewter holders, and even though I'd been caught red-handed with a Cat Stevens tape, I felt my preference for "Hard Headed Woman" and not the simpering, treacly "Moonshadow" exempted me from cliché.

The evening did not end on that pile of carpet. In fact, it was barely evening. The sun was now setting over the hills in the west; sprinklers were sputtering to life as the air cooled; the macabre melody of an ice cream truck was fading into the distance. I was two sheets to the wind, though not yet three. I decided to go for a walk. The best feature of this house was its location, and as I sat in the dark living room that now smelled like carpet glue, I felt I needed to remind myself of that. Not only was the neighborhood lush and bohemian and as imbued with quiet families as it was animated by occasional gun violence, but the street itself was an oasis. Across the road and maybe thirty steps up from the house was that wide, ten-acre slope, an expanse of grasslands upon which, wondrously, no houses had been built. A path had been cleared through the field, and as I approached, my fourth glass of wine in one hand, the dog leash in the other (Rex, for his part, had already ambled off into the distance), I began to experience that particular form of exuberant abandon that comes from walking around drunk in the darkness.

It was a feeling I remembered from New York, when, instead of hailing a cab or taking the subway, I'd often walk thirty or forty blocks home at 1:00 a.m. In the aftertaste of the evening, in the sallow nondarkness of the city night, I'd walk until my feet bloomed with blisters. Passing the panhandlers and the bar crawlers, the bundled-up bus waiters and the uniformed doormen, the lit-up all-night grocery marts and the locked and gated everything else, I could feel the city grazing my cheeks as though a thousand acquaintances were air kissing me at a party. My mood on these walks was always tainted with either vague disappointment or cautious, potentially foolish hope. Maybe I'd have met someone who seemed in possession of some inkling of romantic or sexual possibility, more likely not. Maybe I'd have plunged into deep, revelatory conversation with someone fascinating, more likely not. Still, in the brisk, odorous clutches of the avenues and streets such things mattered less than the physical fact of the city and my ongoing amazement that I'd actually managed to carve out a tiny nook for myself in Manhattan—however dank and costly and echoing with the laughter of richer, happier neighbors. Despite Ridgewood being only twenty miles from Manhattan, the distance between the two places—I'd said it so many times, yet somehow it was never enough—had seemed like an ocean.

And had I now crossed yet another ocean? Was the journey to California equal to or greater than the journey out of Ridgewood, away from Vassar, out of my parents' unending flight from their own pasts? No, not really. Not at all. Sipping my wine, whistling for Rex, I stepped onto the path, where static of all varieties—the scratchy warbles of the first crickets, the rustle of the dog in the grass, the din of distant car alarms and police helicopters and those mysterious pops that are either firecrackers or gunshots—put a hot surge in the fading summer day. Climbing the hill, I experienced a brief moment of Nebraska. For a few seconds, there was nothing before me but grass and sky. I had to catch my breath. I had to bite the inside of my cheek to test for awakeness. One step more, though, and the prairie effect was gone. Rising into view from the crest of the hill were the San Gabriel Mountains to the north, the Hollywood Hills to the west, and the low-slung skyline of Mid-Wilshire to the south-southwest. I sat down on a rock. I called Rex to me and held him close as though he were a teenage boy who'd let me wear his letterman jacket. In the fading light I spotted the Hollywood sign, surreal and cheesy and sublime. Closer in, I saw the undulating, roller-coaster streets of the neighborhood, the haphazard terraces and retaining walls of the properties, my own little house—square and flat roofed and, from certain angles, seemingly befitting of an elf—nestled in its place on my little road.

I saw all this, and it was at once a place I'd never been and a place I'd been all my life. I remember once at college having a dream wherein I was sitting on a log or a rock or some kind of beach staring into blankness, a viewless view. Having suddenly found myself holding a postcard depicting some breathtaking yet nonspecific Arcadian scene, I held it out in front of me, only to have it fuse with my real-life surroundings. It was as if art had been liberated into three-dimensional life, as if some divine force had commanded the worldly and the unworldly to become one. In an instant, by virtue of a single image I'd held in my fingers, I'd made real life join hands with idealized life.

"So what it means," I'd told a friend the next day, "is that my reality answers to my fantasies. I mean, I totally got the feeling from this dream that my life is going to turn out exactly the way I want it. It's like it was saying to me, 'If you picture it, you can get it.' It was like this incredible peace came over me. I could see the road ahead, and it was everything I want."

To which my friend, who was one of those guys who always

accuses others of needing to plan everything out and wanting to settle down rather than have adventures said: "If that's what you want, fine. I guess I'd just rather see where life takes me."

This guy, having once asked me what I wanted from life (no doubt while sitting on his Indian rug listening to Yaz), declared my answer of "contentment" to be "a pity" and "a waste" and "not at all what I want," which, apparently, was a life of "passion, excitement, and rich, fully realized moments that would add up to authentic happiness."

(One of the many tragedies of college life is that it's almost developmentally impossible to have the wisdom to understand that contentment, which implies some sort of sustenance over time, can be an infinitely taller order than happiness, which is often inherently fleeting. It's also unfortunate that your average college student lacks the presence of mind to tell someone to fuck off when he spouts such bong-hit-fueled twaddle about the meaning of "passion.")

I was drunk on the hill. I was not thinking about the conversation about contentment or even the postcard dream. I wasn't thinking about much, since I'd now consumed almost an entire bottle of wine and was instead watching Rex sliver through the grass like a jungle animal, a vision that made me slaphappy until, minutes later, I was suddenly melancholy to the point of tears. It was my first day—my first hours, in fact—as a homeowner, as an evolved human, as a woman who lived not in a sublet or in a condo with wicker and candles but in a real house. And here I was, with a bank loan of $333,701 and an equity line of credit for $71,000 sitting inebriated in an overgrown field trying to hold my imaginary postcard up to the vista before me and see if they fused. Was this the right stop on the road that would give me everything? Was there contentment to be found in these hills, on this street, in that house? Ah yes, I said nearly out loud. This is it! I have it all, I have it all, I have it all!

How did I know this? I didn't, of course. But I do remember that in the midst of this booze-soaked reverie, as I tried to ignore the fact that my legs were getting chewed by some form of menacing no-see-um in the grass and that coyotes—those marauders I'd bragged about in an effort to sound tough— were no doubt watching me from the brush, I allowed myself to drift into the wish that I weren't alone. Though I wanted to be alone at that moment, though I wouldn't have invited any- one up to that hill that night even if I was wearing his ring on my finger, I found myself wondering if I'd ever have a ring on my finger and, if so, how that might or might not change the conditions of the road that gave me everything. Had the house effectively nailed me to one spot on the earth? Would it ward off potential life partners? Or, as per my thinking during the time of crazed house hunting, would it put my best and most authentic self into such high relief that the bad ones would skulk off in fear and the right one would emerge like a card in a magic trick? In other words, did the house look sexy on me? And would I, given my gladly celibate state, ever feel sexy in it?

Unanswerable questions all. Especially when you're dizzy and itchy and your dog is eating coyote dung and you're afraid you're going to trip on a root and break your ankle and have to shout for help, which would be a really bad way to meet the neighbors. Still, as night settled in and Rex, now leashed, pulled me along the path back to the house, a surprising deci- sion came to me. It was surprising not only because it was fully out of the realm of any decision I was making at the time but also because it's not really the kind of thing a person decides. It's the sort of thing you *want* maybe, perhaps even the sort of thing you strongly hope to implement. But that wasn't good enough. There on that hill, in my thirty-fourth year, in my sixth hour of home ownership, I decided that if I ever got married—and that was an *if* and not a *when*—it would be on that hill.

Until I actually signed those escrow papers, the house had been less a visual entity than a contractual one. The first and only time I'd seen it, the day I made my offer, I'd spent maybe five minutes inside the place before zooming down the street with Michael in his Audi TT so we could start the paperwork in his office. Barred from going inside again until I actually took ownership, I'd driven by it a few times with friends and, since it was unoccupied, poked around in the yard and peered in the windows. But even though the yard had continued to be mowed and the hedges trimmed, the house seemed only half there, its pulse faint, its breathing shallow. It also looked smaller every time I went back, though in the catapulting market no one questioned the wisdom of dropping $450,000 on it. The smallest improvements, not to mention the mere passing of weeks, would cause no end of appreciation.

"Here," a friend said, picking up an ugly plastic doormat and depositing it in the trash bin behind the house. "You've just increased the value by $5,000."

Upon moving in, though, I found that the key word was "underwhelming." Following a lazy, artless floor plan reminiscent of a New York City railroad apartment, one room more or less led to the next. The front door opened (abruptly, absent any kind of foyer) into the living room, which led to the kitchen, which led to what was and is the main attraction, a large (by this place's standards) sunporch with vaulted, beamed ceilings, a woodstove, and windows on three sides. Whereas the house itself was built in 1928, this room had been

added in 1983 and apparently not redecorated since. The walls
and ceilings, which were made from cheap, pulpy wood, were
stained dark brown in the vein of faux-wood paneling. A section of what appeared to be redbrick wall behind the fireplace
was actually fake brick face, and the entire floor was covered
with a brown woolly carpet.

The rest of the house was pretty standard stuff. Off the living room (again, no hallways; this was corridor-free living) was
a small bedroom, and off the kitchen was a smaller one. A
small bathroom adjoined them. The kitchen had cheap fake-
marble adhesive tile that was sloppily laid over old linoleum
that had been sloppily laid over subflooring. The bathroom
had not-quite-as-cheap-but-still-awful baby blue tile. The
walls, aside from the barklike rec-room-style walls in the back
room, were either painted a white that had faded to a sallow,
corpselike gray or covered with dark floral wallpaper that,
when I looked closely, I realized would have been best suited
to a Victorian dollhouse, specifically the plastic kind I remember seeing in the Sears catalog in the mid-1970s.

And then there was the garage. I realize that this is the kind
of statement that makes people think women are not equipped
to own property other than full-service condos, but I'll just
come out and say it: I didn't really look at the garage right away
because I was afraid to. But let's understand something: many
a grown man was also afraid of this structure (a weirdly
endearing macho man who I know owns a gun refused to even
approach it; another man told me he wouldn't go near it without a life insurance policy). What wusses, I thought, though
undoubtedly they just thought I was a moron and a sucker.
The garage couldn't be seen from the street or even from the
house itself. The only way to see it was to go beyond the fence
that encloses the "upper" backyard and descend a narrow,

crumbling staircase that drops down from the "lower" back-yard like scary basement steps. (How was it that a house approximately the size of a Chevy Suburban came to have such aristocratic trappings as an "upper" and a "lower" yard? I suspected soil erosion was at least partly to thank.) The stairs were a disaster in their own right; if a major earthquake were to strike when a person was on or near them, the likelihood of being crushed was high. The garage itself, while not without its first-century-European–esque charms, could have conceivably collapsed if a heavy truck rolled by.

The garage was also no longer technically a garage but several tons of concrete carved into a precarious, roofless shell. After the disposal of the ugly doormat, this was my first home improvement. The property had been sold in as-is condition, not least of all because the garage, which was presumably built in 1928 or shortly thereafter, had been completely caved in for decades. Somewhere along the line, the slabs of broken concrete from the roof had even bisected a Volkswagen bus parked inside. Signs reading Danger and No Trespassing were nailed to what remained of a rotted wood fence, and the "driveway," a scabrous stretch of asphalt jutting from a narrow alley, was dusted with the decaying remains of cigarette butts and fast-food containers. At least that's what things looked like when I peeked back there for the first and only time. After I hired a crew of illegal workers to haul the bus and rubble away, what emerged was a sort of hipster homage to both soil erosion and urban decay.

But I had big plans for it. With the proper excavation and construction, it could be rebuilt, and a guesthouse could be added on top. The garage could be new and state-of-the-art and equipped with Peg-Board and shelves and a workbench and room for two cars. And the guesthouse would really be a writing studio with skylights and a sleeping loft and a bathroom and a kitchenette and vast expanses of walls on which enormous pieces of abstract art would hang. Most days, I'd work there uninterrupted (again, everything completed in this space would be prize-worthy), but when guests visited, I'd move my operation inside the house, which would be fine, too. Because they'd be the kinds of guests with busy schedules, they'd be gone much of the day having lunch and attending meetings. But later they'd come back to my place and freshen up in the guesthouse, and by then I'd be finished working, and we'd drink gin and tonics on the patio and then eat dinner under the lemon tree.

For now, though, the walls were crumbling and covered with faded graffiti. I knew enough not to park my car there, but it wasn't as if it had nothing going for it. Actually, it seemed reminiscent of a backdrop in the Anthropologie clothing catalog and therefore kind of sexy—at least in the way an undergraduate art student might appreciate. With a ridiculous, cocky pride that no condo dweller or turnkey property owner would ever know, I lured friends (those who would go, anyway) down the steps and into the garage as though it were a secret garden.

"It's like ancient Rome!" someone said (a kindred spirit, also an art director).

"At least," said someone else, "you've done a nice job with the paint color in the living room."

In home ownership there are two realms: the visible and the invisible, the fun and the unfun, the parts for which there are paint chips and plant nurseries and catalogs filled with doorknobs and drawer pulls and reproductions of Art Deco light fixtures and the parts for which the only gratification is that your water is running and your lights are on. The visible realm is about choices; the invisible realm is about having no choice. The visible realm is about style; the invisible realm is about substance, though it's also about having strange men in your house for long periods of time, after which they will charge you a lot of money for only half solving the problem. During the first year in the house, the visible and the invisible competed with each other like siblings who have nothing in common but their parents. There was no doubt, however, about which one I favored. Though I hired an electrician to install a new circuit panel and wrote endless checks to a plumber who replaced many feet of corroded piping beneath the house, my heart belonged to decorating.

And thus also to *Dwell*. And *House Beautiful* and *Architectural Digest* and *Elle Decor* and *Veranda*. Though more nourishing than the HGTV shows—the pages often emphasized how expensive it can be to do things well rather than how cheap it is to do them shoddily—I imbibed them by the stack and, as with *Trading Spaces* and its ilk, sometimes felt like throwing up afterward. It wasn't just the relentlessness of the magazines, the ubiquity of them, their blockish presence in every doctor's waiting room, every hair salon, every friend's bathroom, that got me down even as I devoured them. It was, for me, the intolerable ache of unmet desire they elicited. Just as in my twenties, the hopelessness of ever living in a majestic West End Avenue prewar had made me want to crumble to the sidewalk as I walked past them, reading *Architectural Digest* proved too much an exercise in self-pity (followed by the requisite guilt for said pity) to devote excessive amounts of time to. Did I really need to read about how a record producer and his vegan chef wife turned their ordinary backyard into a Zen garden with an Infinity pool? Was I doing my brittle ego any favors by exposing it to the smug utterances of an artist couple whose post-and-beam contemporary has not only a living room but also a "conversational pit" and whose carriage house doubles as a studio/gallery/meditation space? If HGTV's genius lay in its ability to entertain viewers while subconsciously making them feel superior to the hapless homeowners on the shows, the perverted success of high-end shelter magazines (like the fashion magazines that spawned them) was that they entertained you while making you hate not only your house but also yourself. And in the words of the inimitable Alison, I could hate myself on my own; I didn't need to contract out for it.

Because here was the thing about my particular approach to home renovation: there was—and still is—really no way to characterize it other than half-assed. Lacking the money to make significant changes in fully committed, significant ways, most of my improvements were minor, low cost, and often only semi-improving. Whereas a more ambitious (or less broke) person might have taken out the ancient and wobbly windows and installed new ones, airtight and secure, I simply covered them with curtains and pretended not to notice how easily someone could break in. Whereas, by all rights, the wood floors should have been out and out replaced, I allowed them to be sanded down to a millimeter of their life and then placed rugs over the spots where they buckled from water damage. Whereas the looming disaster of the retaining wall in the backyard would have kept a more responsible person up at night, I elected to put it out of my mind, instead soothing myself to sleep with visions of dinner parties with calla lilies arcing, dancerlike, out of slender glass vases and hors d'oeuvres served on ceramic trays engraved with Asian designs.

In other words, despite all my exertion in the name of home

repair, I often wasn't repairing as much as I was obscuring. And although this made me feel like a fake and a cheater, it also made me feel as if I were doing *something*. And as I quickly learned, part of the denial that's essential to home ownership is telling yourself that these somethings—even if they're tiny, even if they amount to nothing more than reorganizing the silverware drawer—are ultimately making your house worth, if not more, at least not less than the mind-numbing amount you've paid. If home ownership is little more than a series of denials about how much money you owe to a bank or a mortgage company, such pseudo-improvements are building blocks of these denials. And they make for nice ceramic serving trays, if not necessarily solid windows.

Enlisting any number of chronically tardy, semi- or non-English-speaking painters and floor refinishers and carpenters and handymen, I set about on my various projects. The remainder of the carpet was pulled up and the floor gingerly resanded by a flooring contractor with a finger missing. The living room was painted mint green, the bedroom bright blue, the bathroom butterscotch (I didn't bother with the window or door trim, the scuffed and chipping white paint of which was reminiscent of an Upper West Side prewar and thus signified acceptability). In the back room, I did as much as I could while staying within the bounds of what I could still describe as "nothing too major." Sleek, nickel-plated industrial-style ceiling fans replaced the cheap light fixtures, the concrete floor underneath the brown carpet was polished for a shiny, loftlike effect, and white paint covered every inch of the ceiling and walls, including the fake brick behind the woodstove, which looked considerably less fake that way. Sliding doors leading to the patio were replaced with French doors (this was pretty major, a fact I think I subconsciously tried to deny by buying faux-vintage doorknobs at Anthropologie—yes, the same store whose catalog reminded me of my garage—and ineptly screwing them into the doors in such a way that they did not rotate but merely protruded from either side as if the door had a bone through its nose). Furniture and appliances were bought via Craigslist: a 1930s-era pedestal bathroom sink, four wrought-iron patio chairs, numerous lamps to compensate for my aversion to overhead lights. Other furniture and appliances—the old bathroom sink, the old light fixtures—were sold on Craigslist or deposited by the curb for bulky-item trash collection. After a few months, the mint green living room was repainted terra-cotta, the bright blue bedroom repainted mint green.

The economy and culture of California being what they are, I became an employer not just of intermittent workers but also of regular help. A Mexican gardener named Fernando came every week for $75 a month. A Guatemalan cleaning lady named Marta came twice a month for $80 a pop. Every so often, a nice man (of no discernible ethnic background) from the water softener company came by and replaced the rock salt for a fee of $45. Having decided there was little point in denying my status as a gentrifier, I joined the neighborhood security association, a network of mostly middle- and upper-middle-class homeowners that employed a small stable of private patrol officers to cruise the neighborhood and scare any potential marauders, most of which amounted to kids loitering near the park. For this service I paid $55 a quarter in dues.

In an effort to keep my personal and professional life in concert with the speedy pulse of my home improvement and maintenance efforts, I tried to be social, to be productive, even occasionally to be joyous. I walked Rex in the park and sat on the hill while he nosed around in the grass. I sang Van Morri-

son songs while screwing towel hooks into the bathroom walls
or assembling shelves in the closet. I entertained friends. Alison came over for Thai takeout; eight or ten friends came for
dinner; a crowd of more than seventy-five showed up for an
early October housewarming that spilled from the backyard
into all rooms of the house and jammed the surrounding
streets with cars. I went to the gym, to yoga, to parties, and to
occasional (and still entirely pointless) meetings with movie or
TV executives. I met friends for dinner or for drinks and, on
one occasion, while chatting with the guy on the bar stool next
to me, achieved my goal of looking squarely into an attractive
stranger's eyes and saying, "I own a house." As it happened, so
did he. And it contained his wife and children. This didn't
bother me. Dating him was not the point. Dating in general
was not the point. Despite a vague recollection that I'd
planned to resume dating or at least combing my hair once I
held title and deed on a reasonably well-decorated, furnished,
plumbed, and wired house, I still found myself mired in my
second latency period. The few men who showed interest in
me seemed puerile or psychologically unstable or both. My
hair was still too short and too orange. I had no interest in rec-
tifying these matters.

Indeed, amid the euphoria of my home-ownership dream
realized, a peculiar darkness had set in around me. Though I'd
been counting on the house to make me content—not happy,
of course, but content—the act of taking ownership had somehow done the opposite. It was as if my mood had been goaded
away from situational discontentedness into a dysthymia that
seemed now to be heading into full-fledged depression. In
some ways, though, the word "depression" seems not right.
What I felt, rather, was asleep. At least half-asleep. Somewhere along the line, in between getting references for all

these workmen, calling them, waiting for them to show up, and hearing excuses as to why they didn't (the grand-prize winner in the excuse category: "I had internal bleeding"), something had happened to my brain that felt not unlike light anesthesia. It wasn't that I was unhappy or angry or wanting anything to be different. It was more that I was beginning to feel an unsettling torpor lining the contours of my existence, a sense of neutrality that was only exacerbating my neutered physical essence and slowly pushing me toward a state of being in which my favorite activity, aside from monitoring antique light fixture auctions on eBay, was turning in for the night with Rex. Whether or not it was cold, I preferred he sleep not at the foot of the bed but next to me, preferably with his head on a pillow.

Was I working during this time? Yes. Sort of, anyway. I was teaching the aforementioned graduate writing course at an art college about fifty miles north of L.A., a gig that required me to hold forth on subjects such as "narrative arc" for three hours a week, plus read a lot of student work, much of it about sexual fetishes. I also have a magazine clip or two from this period, so it appears that I hadn't retired. But my output was minimal to say the least. Did I socialize? Again, my memory of this time is abstruse and slightly surreal, the cognitive manifestation of a finger poking through cotton at the top of an aspirin bottle, but I think I did see friends. I'm pretty sure, however, that I did so for the sole purpose of talking about my house. I know I talked about nothing other than the house in one of my meetings with film executives since my agent called afterward and said only, "I hear you changed your mind about the color of the living room." Needless to say, I didn't get a development deal or whatever it was I was supposedly in there to get. In fact, it was one of my last "industry meetings." My agent—understandably, mercifully—moved on to other clients. I moved on from the cumbersome lie of pretending I was interested in anything other than the acquisition of the perfect set of wall sconces. With friends, I no longer bothered with conversational throat clearing. There was no "How are you? What have you been up to?" Just "What do you know about bathtub caulk?"

"You're allowed to stay on this topic for six months," Alison told me (she of the full-service condo with the tiny terrace and the Jacuzzi tub and appliances so new that even a nuclear attack would not interrupt the spin cycle; she who didn't know what it meant to able to smell your electricity). "You're beginning to bore people. Maybe you should try going on a date."

Of course, what I knew but had not yet brought myself to fully articulate was that I was on a twenty-four-hour-a-day, seven-day-a-week date with my house and had no room for any other relationship. Three months, four months, six months into my home ownership, and I still had a moratorium on pleasures of the flesh or even the prefatory pleasures of being taken out to dinner. In fact, this moratorium had gradually extended into a moratorium on things I'd once assumed myself incapable of not doing: working, socializing, reading.

But there I was, not doing them. I was not, in fact, doing anything. At night (and, admittedly, for much of the day) I would sit at my desk in the rec-room-turned-loftlike space and stare at the industrial-style ceiling fan above my head until I felt I could almost rise up into it and allow the blades to cut fine slices off the top of my scalp. Other times I would lie in bed for more than an hour in the late afternoon, watching dusk float through the windows and settle into the house like a tranquilizer. Los Angeles has magic-hour lighting that literally has the effect of allowing one to see the world through a rose-tinted glass, and from my bed this display looked marvelous, even somehow culturally significant. It was as if the house demanded that I be there as a witness to its fleeting moments of beauty. And I, having increasingly nowhere to go and nothing to do, was happy to obey. This was no longer light anesthesia. This was a coma.

If there is anything I pride myself on, it's dental and mental hygiene. I've never had a cavity, nor have I ever found myself unable to cope with most of what comes up in the life of a person of my particular station. By the time I acquired my house, I'd figured out how to earn a living, how to unclog the toilet, when to rotate my car tires, when to take something to the dry cleaner. I had, back at age thirty, realized that loose-fitting tops are best paired with streamlined bottoms and vice versa (at twenty-seven I did not know this). I could cook dinner for friends (nothing haute cuisine, but passable), walk into crowded parties by myself, speak in front of large audiences, and take long international flights without drugging myself or worrying excessively about losing my passport. But the year I became a homeowner, my teeth continued to thrive while something else eroded. My grip on my own humanity was loosening. There is no way to explain it other than I seemed to be allergic to both the outside world and myself. I couldn't stand being alone in my house and yet could not bear to be around most people. It was as if the pleasure in solitude that had once worked so well in my favor had become a foul-tasting compulsion, the toxic centerpiece of my life.

When I look back on 2004, I see a downward curve that appears to reach its nadir somewhere around August, just a month after I bought the house. It then gives the impression of remaining steady until well into December until, like a plane in an imperceptible spiral dive, it reveals itself to have been plummeting steadily the whole time. That is to say, even when I thought I was getting better or at least staying the same, I was actually getting worse. As bad as I felt around Labor Day, when I'd be in a supermarket and suddenly feel such an urgent need to get home and lie on the bed, Thanksgiving was worse than I even perceived it at the time. Having eschewed all invitations in favor of quiet quality time alone at the house, I'd convinced myself that I was elated and proud to be cooking a box of Stove Top stuffing and eating it while actually *sitting at the kitchen table* rather than standing over the sink. How civilized I was! (There was that word again; it haunted me.) How peaceful and empowered and possessed of such comfort in my own skin it was as if I were wearing pajamas. As it happened, I actually was wearing pajamas.

What was happening here, really? Was this simply a homeowner's version of postpartum depression? Was I suffering the inevitable disappointment of getting what you wish for? I think I might have suspected as much at the time, but now I wonder if my malaise had to do with something slightly different. I wonder if it was not the uprooting that had thrown me off balance but, rather, the disorienting effects of staying put. This was, after all, the first time in nearly three years that I hadn't been actively trying to move. If life in the Silver Lake farmhouse had been marked by intense decorating followed by intense house hunting, if life before then had been a lurching migration from broken lease to sublet to doomed farm purchase to another broken lease to a dogsit, life on Escalada Terrace must have seemed frighteningly static at first, even suffocating. Over the years, transience had become my default setting. If I wasn't moving, I was making plans to move. And now that those hobbies had been taken away, now that looking and thinking about real estate qualified more as a sick indulgence than as a survival mechanism, I found myself stripped not only of a pastime but also of a purpose. I quite literally did not know what to do with myself.

How does one pull out of such a spiral dive? The short answer: by running out of money to the point where you have no choice but to go back to work. I'll have you know this: I got a temp job. I got a gig writing catalog copy for an international diet food company. Instead of meeting with producers in Hollywood, I started getting in the car every morning at eight and driving to an office building I accessed with a key card I wore around my neck. I then sat at a desk until 6:00 p.m. every night, typing out things like "Jan feels great and has tons of energy, but results may vary" and showing them to an editor who would give me back notes like "sounds too breezy." Maybe the workplace was so depressing that I couldn't help but feel less depressed at home. Maybe, in the true spirit of my Midwestern roots, I was simply better off toiling away in mindless if income-generating drudgery than staring at my wall waiting for inspiration to descend from above like a sudden leak. In any case, I got better, though I can't give you the long answer as to why. The long answer is something I'll probably never be able to articulate, because I'll probably never have it. The long answer, I suspect, is inexpressible because it never really comes. Like growing up or honestly falling in or out of love, the journey to sane from not entirely sane traverses an invisible plain. You can no more know how or when you got better than know how or when you came unglued in the first place.

I do have one strong suspicion, though. I think my bathroom floor might actually have cured me. By now it was early 2005. I still hadn't gone on a date or anything, but my hair had gone back to blond, and it was not quite as short. The condition and decor of the house, though not perfect, were decent.

One night while brushing my teeth before bedtime, I noticed that a tiny, hexagon-shaped piece of porcelain tile was peeking up from a missing corner of the cheap and hideous baby blue vinyl tile. Though I'd seen this porcelain before, somehow I'd never registered it as *the* porcelain, *the* original hexagonal porcelain tile from 1928 that, in my imagination and (I knew for a fact; over the years I'd become as sure of this as I was of my own name) in *many people's imaginations,* represents not just tile or floor covering but an entire life philosophy, an entire aesthetic system, an entire way of—there is no other way to put it—being okay in the world.

How had I not noticed it before? I think I had but subconsciously assumed it was a lost cause. I'm pretty sure I'd thought that underneath that baby blue layer of Landlord's Delight lay the shards of the house's most delicate bones. I'd figured the tiles were broken and that coming face-to-face with the senseless damage would serve only to press further down on the bruise that had become my only mood. But that evening—and it was late, nearly eleven; well past my bedtime—I took a butter knife and set about prying up the vinyl tile as though a miner were trapped beneath it. And to my amazement, in tiny fragments and, occasionally, in large, fist-sized sections, the stuff peeled off the floor, revealing inch after inch of perfectly intact white porcelain tiles. A filthy layer of impossibly sticky adhesive covered every inch, of course, and my pants ripped at the knees and my shoes stuck to the floor and, by the third hour, my clothes were soaked with sweat and my nails were broken and my hands were bleeding and my right thumb was virtually paralyzed from gripping the knife so hard.

By 3:00 a.m. I had a new bathroom floor. Because this floor was composed of original porcelain hexagonal tile, I had a new life. Or maybe it was just the opposite. Maybe I had my old life back. The tiles that had captured my imagination so many years ago—in the music copyist's apartment (and I hadn't even seen them there, hadn't even known what they were; I'd merely intuited their presence and subconsciously identified them as my own personal meme), in the apartment on 100th Street, in the apartment on Eighty-sixth Street—had formed the path that led me, finally, to this home of my own. In unearthing them, perhaps I had unearthed missing pieces of myself, the pieces that had been lost along all the moves like wayward china or that box of random, uncategorizable items (extra keys, silk flowers, a twelve-roll pack of paper towels) that inevitably never makes it from point A to point B. And now here they were. And here I was, perhaps finally greater than, or at least equal to, the sum of the parts I'd strewn across the country over all the moves. Here I was, finally unpacking my stuff with no intention of repacking it. And as though I'd been reintroduced to a favorite song that the years had erased from my brain, my spirits lurched back into their sockets. My house had almost ruined me until it pulled me, like a piece of driftwood, back to the rock-ribbed shore.

SIX

Time passed. It's an obvious thing to say, but sometimes it's the only thing to say. Finally, my house and I made peace. I quit picking at it, and it quit sprouting leaks and emitting strange buzzing noises. That is to say, I paid people to fix the leaks and stop the buzzing noises and finally got busy with other things. My days, dull as ever, were at least not sacrificed to catatonia. I went to my temp job at the diet food company, I went to yoga, I went home and did not watch *Trading Spaces* or *House Hunters* or *Design on a Dime* but read the newspaper—and sometimes actual books—instead. Eventually, I began writing occasional arts and entertainment articles for the *Los Angeles Times* (admittedly, one was about a design show called *Monster House*), and when presented with the opportunity to try out for a position as a weekly columnist on the opinion page, I stayed up late at night after the temp job and wrote as if my life depended on it.

Actually, it was my house that depended on it. The mortgage payment was $2,054 per month. This did not include payments on the equity line of credit I'd run up with all the floor refinishing and electrical panel replacing and painting. I couldn't get by on diet food money alone. And then the *L.A. Times* gave me the column. I was now going to write something every week that really had nothing to do with real estate or home decor (not that I didn't sneak it in whenever possible). Instead, I wrote about what I called "social politics," about the intersection of hard news and pop culture, about abortion rights and gay marriage and Madonna and Ann Coulter and fires in Malibu. This wasn't a full-time job, and it didn't pay enough to keep my whole ship afloat, but it did allow me to quit the diet food company so I could take on other freelance assignments and devote my whole work schedule to writing. And like a stalker who finally begins to lose interest in the object of his obsession, I began to think about things other than real estate and whether the green walls in the bedroom were still not the right shade of green. Sure, there were half-assed renovations I still wanted to do in, for instance, the kitchen. But I put them out of my mind. Instead of thinking about home improvements every day, I thought about them every week, then maybe twice a month. I began to get a life. And then—because apparently that's how these things work— I met a man neither puerile nor psychologically unstable.

His name was Alan. I liked the name. It reminded me of the 1970s somehow, also of upper West End Avenue in New York. A bearded guy wearing a corduroy jacket over a turtleneck, reading *Dissent* as he waited for a Broadway bus circa 1975, could have been named Alan. But this one was young. One year younger than I am, in fact. He was also mysterious, weird, tall, long eyelashed, wry, a goofball. He was a science reporter at the paper. We met in the lobby, where we were both waiting to meet up with a small group of writers and editors going out for dim sum in Chinatown. It turned out we lived near each other—he was a few miles away in Silver Lake, very near my old rental place—and had once even lived near each other in New York (I on West Eighty-sixth, he on West Ninetieth). But that's not the point. The point is that within five minutes of starting to talk to him, I recognized something so familiar it was almost as if I were catching a whiff of some beloved, comforting scent from long ago.

What I was smelling was pure impermanence, the pheromonal emanations of a man on the move. This guy was the epitome of a flight risk, an advertisement for not calling after the third date, or the first. A former expatriate in several countries and pretty clearly a settle-down-a-phobe of the highest order, he had a relocation history that made my moves look like merely rolling around a lot in bed. He'd lived in Uganda and Rwanda, in New York, Mexico City, and Palo Alto, and in a portable ice hut, he claimed, in Washington State. He spoke English and Spanish and some Swahili. He'd done the kind of moving where you show up in a foreign land with a duffel bag and some friend of a friend's phone number scribbled on a napkin and the kind where your company packs you up and flies you out and sets you up in a gated house with a maid and a secretary. He was a pro.

Unlike mine, Alan's transience seemed born more out of curiosity—and sometimes genuine professional necessity—than out of neurotic compulsion. He'd grown up in one house—a comfortable, upper-middle-class split-level in a solid, wholesome rust-belt city—and had parents who were no more interested in moving than they would have been in the state of contemporary fiction if such a thing had ever crossed their minds. In other words, he was both a citizen of the world and a homegrown American boy. He was the human equivalent of a farmstead in the middle of a major city. And, in a refreshing change of pace from much of the last few years, when he asked me out, I was actually intrigued.

My house must have sensed competition. Less than an hour before my first date with Alan, a Saturday brunch in Silver Lake, I stepped out of the shower and found that the water would not turn off. Though the faucet knob itself turned (360 degrees in fact, like an owl rotating its head), the water flow was unaffected by this action and was gushing into the bathtub at something resembling six gallons per minute. That in and of itself may have posed more of an environmental hazard than a potential structural calamity if not for the fact that the bathtub drain was about 95 percent stopped up. The water produced by a five-minute shower usually took about an hour and a half to empty out of the tub. I'm embarrassed to say that this had been going on for the entire time I'd been in the house (nearly two years), and despite my attempts to remedy the problem with Drano and with wire coat hangers and, at one point early on, by enlisting the help of the handyman who'd had internal bleeding, it remained unfixed.

So there I was forty minutes before my date: the water hurling forth and rising menacingly toward the surface, the faucet handle broken, and no idea how to turn the water main off. I realize these are the anecdotes out of which escrow papers that say "——, an unmarried woman," are born. I know being a single female homeowner who doesn't know how to turn off the water main in her own home is tantamount to being a sexually active teenager who believes you can't get pregnant on a Thursday. I remember smiling and condescendingly shaking my head when Kim, back in Lincoln, recounted the story of buying her house and then having to call her father, who lived in a town fifty miles away, because she couldn't figure out how to open her garage door. I no longer shake my head at that story, at least not condescendingly. In fact, whenever I think of that story now, I think, "How lucky that she had a garage."

But back to the water main. I called the Department of Water and Power and got a recording. The bathtub was now just inches from overflowing, so I got a bucket and started scooping water into the toilet. Finally, with ten minutes until the date, I called the cell number Alan had given me.

"I have a leak," I said. This was technically a lie, but it sounded better than the multifaceted and therefore rather farcical truth.

"Do you need help?" he asked.

"Oh, no. No, 'no, no, no. I can totally fix it. I'll be there as soon as I can. I just might be a little late."

"Why don't I stop by?" he asked.

"Oh, no!" I said passive aggressively. "No, no, no, no. That's too much to ask."

"What's your address?" he asked.

"It's okay, no!"

"No, really."

"Really?"

"Really."

As it happened, I found the water shutoff before he arrived, though not before I ransacked the clothes hamper—suddenly there was nothing in the closet, not a stitch of acceptable clothing—and wedged my perspiring body into a sundress, a cardigan, and flip-flops (the official uniform of brunch in L.A. in March—or all the other months, for that matter), and rubbed concealer on a blooming forehead zit. Then I made one last survey of the side of the house, spotted an iron handle connected to a copper pipe, and yanked it to one side. The whisper of running water groaned into silence. Success. I then looked up and saw a Volvo station wagon turning around on the hill and sliding to a stop against the curb. Alan got out of the car. He was wearing torn jeans and a sweatshirt with a stain on it.

"I fixed it!" I yelped in a manner that I hoped would convey self-sufficiency without mannishness. "Totally fixed. Sorry to make you come all the way out here. Totally fixed. Wasn't that big a deal, actually."

"That's too bad," he said, small starbursts of crow's-feet emerging from his eyes as he smiled. "I like to fix things. Maybe you could break it again."

Don't worry, this book is not about to career headlong into Sandra Bullock–movie territory. I'm not about to write, "And then I met a real man who knew how to swing a hammer, and he rescued me from the money-hemorrhaging pathos of my lonely, helpless existence and, along the way, showed me that a house isn't a home until you share it with someone or at least have decent insulation." I'm not going there, at least not totally. Alan may have been a guy who liked to fix things (also evidently a guy who wore stained sweatshirts on first dates), but he was also a journalist, a dedicated endurance athlete, and an inveterate outdoorsman (unlike those of most drivers in Los Angeles, the racks on top of his car had actually been used). He had too many interests to really shape up to be the kind of guy who rescues a single, home-owning woman from the burdens of her solitude and broken faucets. And that was okay, since I didn't want to be saved.

If anything, something about him invited a return to the old obsessions. During that first brunch, I had become possessed of a need to look at hardware for kitchen cabinets. The restaurant happened to be down the street from the architectural salvage store—a cavernous, chaotic warehouse where massive stone fireplaces and entire entryways from now-demolished Victorians were packed together like refugees in a camp—and I now entreated him to accompany me there so I could look at drawer and cabinet pulls. Alan seemed confused by this errand, particularly the urgency with which I appeared to need these seemingly junklike items.

"What do you think?" I asked him, holding two nearly identical tarnished-brass drawer pulls in my hand. "This one or that one? This one kind of looks like something that should be on a mailbox, but the other one looks like it got caught in a tornado."

"Are these really better than the ones you have now?" Alan asked.

Silly man. Of course they weren't! But no matter. What mattered was that in the time it had taken us to eat brunch and talk about various people we knew and books we'd read and National Public Radio shows we secretly found annoying, the vague interest I'd lately been harboring in making some improvements to my kitchen had transformed into an exigency. Though it had been nearly a year since I'd undertaken a domestic project more involved than rearranging the coat closet (which also housed the washer and dryer, hot water heater, and five shelves of office supplies and music CDs), my yen to replace the linoleum in the kitchen with wood floors and redo the early-1980s fiberboard cabinets so they looked—alas—like worn-down original cabinets in an early-twentieth-century farmhouse was no longer a yen. It was an itch I had to scratch right then and there.

This idea for the floor and cabinets had come to me while flipping through a catalog. Not the Restoration Hardware catalog, not the Sundance catalog (which is nothing if not a paean to early-twentieth-century farmhouses with their original, worn-down cabinets), not even *Architectural Digest* or *Elle Decor* or *Dwell*. No, the periodical from whose pages this bolt of design-on-a-much-more-than-a-dime inspiration struck was not a home-furnishing catalog at all but rather a clothing catalog for a company called Soft Surroundings. Specializing in long jackets and tunics and flowing pants in exotic, Asian-inspired prints, Soft Surroundings caters to that particular category of women who are well into middle age but whose sartorial predilections remain so rooted in early-1970s earth-mother-esque bohemia (peasant blouses, ankle-length batik dresses, knit ponchos) that they are all but incapable of wearing solid colors or anything with a zipper.

Soft Surroundings takes this aesthetic and makes it a little more age appropriate for forty- to sixty-something women and also blander in a sort of glazed-over, Midwestern way (there's a single, flagship store in St. Louis). In other words, even though the models are young and smooth-skinned and have the same jutting collarbones of all catalog models, it's pretty clearly a catalog for women of a certain age. And while I didn't at that point consider myself a woman of any age other than the one I was (I was thirty-six), I do admit being drawn into the Soft Surroundings catalog in a rather embarrassing and even perplexing way. There was one particular ballet top that I liked so much I purchased it in six different colors. I also ordered a long, embroidered jacket with a Japanese-style collar that was entirely too big for me even in extra small (one of the seductions of the catalog is self-delusion engendered by its enormous sizes) and, I later realized, made me look like the "artsy grandma" on a Lipitor commercial. The fact that I was wearing this jacket when I met Alan and the fact that he asked me out anyway still strikes me as something close to a presidential pardon.

The most money I ever spent thanks to Soft Surroundings, however, was the result of an image on a single page of the spring 2006 catalog. On this page, a woman in the ballet top, a long flowered skirt, and sandals stands in a kitchen. You can't see much of the kitchen, but you can see that the floors are a blond wood and the walls are yellow and the cabinets are an off-white with a sort of distressed, peeling-paint quality. The handles appear to be tarnished brass. The model is of course very pretty and thin and collarbony. Were she a real person, she'd undoubtedly be the kind of person who was loved deeply by whomever she shared that kitchen with.

After the date with Alan, I called the floor guy with the missing finger. I called the painters. I called a neighbor around the corner who was a carpenter and detail painter who—wouldn't you know—specialized in making new stuff look old. I showed him the page from the Soft Surroundings catalog and said, "Do this; just like this." The floor installers (overseen by the missing-finger guy, who, unlike a few years earlier, when he would have done the work himself, now apparently had bigger fish to fry than my little house) didn't show up the first few times and then showed up late. They tracked mud into the house and left Mountain Dew bottles in the yard. They said it would take one week; then they said it would take three. Missing-finger guy had originally said the cost would be $2,500. Then it was likely going to be $3,000, maybe $3,200.

All the while, I told Alan, who'd asked me out again and then a third time, not to come over. Not just yet. Not for a week or so. Better to hang out at his place, which was more convenient to restaurants and the movie theater and the gelato shop and all the places that couples go when they've just met and something as prosaic as gelato can make you think the world is singing to you. Better to hang out at his place, though, admittedly, it was a bit of a shit hole. Not that it didn't show good instincts on his part. In the lower-level apartment of a dark, drafty sixty-year-old wood-sided house, he'd thrown Persian and Mexican rugs over the dark pine floors and picked up a round, mission-style oak dining table at a flea market that now sat, entirely covered in papers, in a cobwebby corner. The living room and an adjacent office were home to not only hundreds of books, newspapers, and outdated issues of *The Atlantic, The New Yorker, The Economist,* and *The New York Review of Books* but also a bicycle, two surfboards, countless pairs of running shoes, two pairs of skis, a pair of swim fins, a box of rock-climbing gear, and a coatrack choked with wetsuits, rain apparel, snow apparel, wind apparel, and a Medusan tangle of bungee cords. Against the wall by the front door, a pile of newspapers rose to nearly five feet. In addition to that, the sofa, the floor, the bed, and the area surrounding the bed were festooned with at least three months' worth of *The New York Times Magazine,* the cover folded over the back and the crossword puzzles in various stages of completion.

Lacking a dishwasher or even a decent sponge, Alan often left his dirty plates, sticky with spaghetti and stir-fried vegetables and ice cream, in the sink and walked away with seemingly no further plans for them. He did this even though the house had a tremendous moth problem; they'd periodically invade the cupboards and bore through the rice and flour bags like termites.

"Shouldn't we do the dishes?" I asked once.

"Nah, the cleaning lady's coming," he said.

"Oh! Tomorrow?"

"Next week."

Back at home, three weeks of work on the kitchen turned into four and a half weeks. This was due not to the extent of the job, which was minimal, but to the lack of regularity with which anyone showed up to do it. On days when someone came, I'd rejoice. I'd provide coffee. On other days, I'd seethe. I'd call them one by one: the floor guy, the painters, my carpenter neighbor, who, to be fair, had a much better-paying gig going in Malibu and was trying his best to squeeze my cabinets in on the side.

"When will you be finished?" I asked them all like a child whining "Are we there yet?" in the car. "Please, please finish!" Here I was with a new boyfriend—at least he seemed to be going in the direction of boyfriend; he'd called after the third date and also the fourth and the sixth—and I couldn't show him my house, which, to my mind, amounted to not showing him half of my face. Meanwhile, I wrote my newspaper column amid hideous banging and drilling and ranchero music. "Please finish! What can I do to move this along?" I implored a worker who was prying up the last shards of what turned out to be four layers of linoleum on the kitchen floor. He spoke no English. I, shamefully, spoke no Spanish. I might as well have been asking, "What can I do to make it rain?"

Eventually they finished. They always finish. Barring some kind of force majeure in the manner of an entire construction crew developing internal bleeding or, of course, running out of money or credit, these things really do come to an end. It's just that when it comes to home improvement—even, maybe especially, for noncommittal renovators like myself—the finale is often strangely anticlimactic. There's always one tiny thing left to do. There's always one irregularly sized screw or washer or piece of pipe that needs to be special ordered and that Pete or Sal or José will return with and install just as soon as it comes in. Maybe because once it's finished you're faced with the dull tasks of moving the furniture back, returning the food to the cupboards, making dinner and cleaning it up, and then making it again the next night. Maybe that's because the process of home improvement is so punishing that even the most magnificent outcome, even a kitchen or yard or addition that makes your friends smolder with envy, was probably such a hell ride to actually get done that the final unveiling can only be underwhelming. All that mess and noise and money for *this*? Three permits and two inspections and some really pissed-off neighbors for *this*?

I knew, of course, that this kitchen work was a shining exemplar of my neither-here-nor-there renovation style. Granted, the floor was unquestionably improved, but there were no new appliances or counters, no reconfiguring of the cupboards, just some yellow paint on the wall, some rusty antique hardware, and some cabinets made to look weathered. If I'd been a set decorator—or, indeed, a production designer for backdrops in the Soft Surroundings catalog—I'd have done my job to perfection. In real-life terms, however, the endeavor ultimately seemed lacking. Perhaps that's why I'd suddenly set my sights on the guest room as well, issuing a last-minute directive to the workers to remove the dark, Victorian dollhouse wallpaper and replace it with a coat of white paint. The goal was to make the room look slightly less like a chamber in which a depressed poet might try to kill herself with arsenic. But somehow instead the white walls made the place look even more foreboding. A minuscule six by eight feet, the room had a single window that looked out onto a cement retaining wall. The only views of anything came from the television set, which, since I'd moved in, I'd watched in that room while sitting on a stack of blankets on the floor. A disproportionately large ceiling fan with a tinted pink globe over the light had hung from the ceiling for the first year until one day I'd reached over my head to take off my sweater and knocked it to the floor, where it shattered. Since then, a bare bulb had hung from the filthy fan like something from an interrogation chamber.

How was my new boyfriend—or my potential new boyfriend, or my future boyfriend, or whatever he was—supposed to come over and watch TV in a room like this?

This solution, I feared, meant only one thing: getting reacquainted with that old trope from my Vassar days, a futon. This time with a frame.

Sure, I could have upgraded to a sofa bed, but I'm not sure that constitutes an upgrade. Something about sofa beds seemed corroded somehow, even crime scene–ish, as though at any given time you could unfold that sorry little mattress and find a dead body, or at the very least an ancient and rotting sandwich. Futons, on the other hand, had a crispness that almost made up for their uniform ugliness. Futons signified youth and exuberance. Futons, as loath as I was to be resorting to one at the age of thirty-six, brought me back to the days of hoping their promise of sex and roomy slumber would result in the acquisition of a boyfriend and, barring that, at least knowing I was strong and spry enough to move one up and down a flight of stairs without assistance.

This futon, naturally, would be different. It would be different because I was fifteen years older than I'd been back in those days and the ramifications of the thing were entirely different. How did I know this? For one thing, I found one that barely even looked like a futon. Far removed from those faux-Scandinavian, mass-produced, slatted pine benches you see in a million advertisements in *The Village Voice,* this futon actually sort of looked like an antique. In fact, with its wrought-iron frame and dark purple velvet-covered cushion it looked vaguely Moroccan, a Moroccan antique! It would match the mosaic coffee table and bed stands (not that any of those things fit in the guest room). It would do the job of a futon without reducing the house to Dani-caliber shoddiness. No scented candles would be casting a sorry glow on this futon. Hell, no one would even know it was a futon. People would think I'd bought it for $10,000 in one of the furniture showrooms on La Brea Avenue.

At least this was my assumption as I drove to get it. The place I was driving to was not a furniture showroom or even an antiques store but rather the Hollywood apartment of someone named Margaret who was selling it on Craigslist. Based on the photos, I'd assumed it was such a coveted piece that it might be snatched up before I could complete the seven-mile drive from Escalada Terrace. "Don't sell it to anyone else!" I'd spastically typed to Margaret in an e-mail. "I'm coming over immediately. Leaving right now! This futon was made for me to lie on."

The futon, it turned out, was made for a large bag of granite to lie on. Six feet long, two and a half feet deep with arms and legs like pylons, it was a mighty, if not exactly Moroccan, piece. Margaret, who had to be out of her apartment the next day because she'd broken up with her live-in boyfriend and couldn't pay the rent, didn't exactly remember how to open it into a bed but promised it was possible and that there were no sandwiches inside. Though I wasn't as in love with the real thing as I'd been with the pictures, it still seemed well above average as far as futons were concerned, so I wrote her a check for $250. Then I went home and got back on Craigslist to find a man with a van who'd pick it up at Margaret's and deliver it to me for an additional $100. The transaction seemed costly and cumbersome, especially for a piece of used furniture, but as a frequent Craigslist shopper I was used to this, and, besides, I was so eager to finally invite my new maybe-boyfriend into my newly improved house that I didn't care if there was a sandwich in the mattress. I just wanted to open the front door for Alan and show him something that might make him feel like staying awhile.

The delivery guys came right on time. Like all man-with-van guys on Craigslist, they both looked like a cross between a homeless meth addict and a wildebeest. They banged and scraped the thing up the walkway through the front door and into the living room, where they paused and mopped their brows and stunk like Drum tobacco and, like anyone who'd ever delivered anything to Escalada Terrace, cursed about the steepness of the street. Then they picked it up again, inched it into the kitchen door, and turned toward the guest room door.

"Right in there will be fine," I said. I was wearing one of the ballet tops from Soft Surroundings—the taupe one—and san-dals and a long skirt and standing next to my distressed wood cabinets drinking a glass of lemonade. In just a matter of min-utes, my tableau would be complete.

"It ain't gonna fit in there," said one wildebeest. "The door is too narrow. It won't make the corner."

"Really?" I said. "Surely there's a way!"

They box stepped around it for a few minutes. We moved the table. We moved the refrigerator. They turned the futon sideways and upright and upside down.

"Not gonna happen," the other wildebeest said. "Didn't you measure it when you bought it?"

"Of course I measured inside the room," I said. "I measured to see if it would fit against the wall."

Meghan Daum, an unmarried woman. Meghan Daum, an unmarried woman.

"Well, it don't fit," said the first wildebeest, taking a cigarette out of his pocket even though he was still balancing the hulking, clanking metal frame on its side with one hand. "There's no way it'll go in."

They left the futon on its side in the kitchen, leaning against the doorway. I paid them the $100—they hadn't finished the job, but they didn't seem like the types to argue with—and they walked out of the house and sputtered down Escalada Terrace in their van, the sound of heavy-metal music streaming behind them like exhaust. Inside, the futon stood nearly seven feet tall with the extra inches of its enormous iron armrests. It looked down at me like a menacing machine in some rancid factory; it mocked me with its wheezing springs and terrifying hinges. I stared back at it. I looked at my new floor and my new painted guest room and thought about Alan. I could have called him, I suppose. I could have waited for him to come over the next day and, upon ushering him into the kitchen, ratcheted my voice up an octave and said, "So, uh, wanna help me with this?"

But no. I would not do that. I would not ruin the big reveal. Furthermore, I would not relinquish autonomy over my house to a guy who might not even be my boyfriend yet, a guy who seemed interested enough in me but who any day could get a reporting assignment in Papua New Guinea and decide to just move there and live in a tree house with a supermodel turned Médecins sans Frontières doctor. No! I was not going to let that happen. Not after all the house and I had been through together. I changed out of my Soft Surroundings outfit and into a T-shirt, shorts, and (for lack of steel-toed boots) running shoes. This was going to be a long night.

I'm still not quite sure how I got that thing inside the guest room. To this day, I remain convinced that the dimensions of the doorway are smaller than those of the futon. But I can tell you it took seven hours of pushing, pulling, sliding, scraping, hoisting, cursing, and screaming (with several breaks in between to eat and/or throw tantrums) until finally, miraculously, possibly even mathematically impossibly, it was in there. And after I somehow managed to lower all eight hundred pounds off its side and onto four legs without breaking my fingers or sending it crashing through the floor, I felt more triumphant than I had since the evening of the porcelain tile excavation. Once again, I was filthy, bloodied, and drenched. Once again, I'd spent an entire evening doing an incredibly prosaic task in the most arduous way possible. But it was done, the goal achieved. Buoyed by the adrenaline of victory, I lay down on the futon and fell into an incandescent sleep.

Did I dream? I'd like to say so. I'd like to say I dreamed of an extra room or of a house that was free to someone deserving, a house not free in monetary terms but free in spirit, with its doors and windows open and no sharp edges between inside and outside, no secret passwords for entry, no layers of pedigreed lineage required for cosigning. But I'm pretty sure I just passed out and spent the night as lifeless and brain-dead as a bag of granite. When I awoke, my back and shoulders felt as if they'd been slammed into the hood of a car. My big toe was blackened. The newly painted doorframe was gashed on one side. Stumbling into the kitchen, I beheld the gleaming wood floors, the cheery yellow walls, the sylvan anti-burnish of the cabinets. All together, this enterprise, including the futon delivery, had cost me nearly $4,000.

The newspaper thumped against the walkway. I ambled outside, barely dressed—a regular habit since the only neighbors within eyeshot were late risers (or so I chose to believe). Streaks of morning light were unfolding over the hill across the street. The purple martins were warbling from the lemon tree. A scrawny dog—no, a coyote—swaggered right up the street, stealthy and coy as a gangster, and headed back to its den in the creases of the hill. This is a great house, I thought to myself. With or without the new kitchen floors, with or without the futon, this was not a house without considerable virtues. This was a house of integrity and character, a modest house but also, in its own way, a commanding one. It deserved to be met on its own terms. It had needed some improving, but it also deserved its share of uncomplicated, unprodding, unintervening affection. I owed it—and somehow I was only realizing this now—at least that much. I owed it my love, not just my scrutiny.

That evening Alan came over. "Finally!" I said, as if to imply his nonvisitation hadn't been at my behest, as if to imply he just hadn't bothered until now (he saw through this, no doubt, but graciously went along with it). I gave him the twelve-second tour. I feigned nonchalance about the kitchen floors and the farmhouse cabinets and the guest room and the velvet and wrought-iron futon. I led him through the back room with the polished concrete floors and the whitewashed walls and the nickel-plated ceiling fans, through the French doors, and out to the backyard.

I brought him a beer. I made some kind of mediocre dinner—spaghetti or rosemary chicken or defrosted salmon wrapped in foil—and we ate outside on the patio furniture I'd purchased from Craigslist a year earlier. We trod lightly into talk about the demons of our parents and the oddness of our siblings and the various calamities of our previous relationships— the things people talk about on the eighth or ninth date, the things they save until there's a modicum of safety. And as I led him through the yard to show him the view from over the fence, as I explained the particular nighttime wonder of the twinkling, terraced houses and the strangely comforting searchlights of police helicopters and the fact that occasionally an owl would fly down from the park and sit on a branch like a watchman, Alan stopped beneath the orange tree. Plucking a ripe one, he began peeling it, the rind shaving off into a perfect ribbon.

"This is a great house," he said.

SEVEN

In 2006, the year I met Alan and two years after I'd bought the house on Escalada Terrace, something called Zillow came along. Zillow is a Web site that calculates the estimated value of your home (there's that word again, "home"— as if something essentially abstract could be measured by some kind of computerized algorithm). The idea is that it tells you how much your property is worth based on recent sales figures for comparable properties. This is called the Zillow "Zestimate." Of course, the Zestimate is famously misleading, because it has no way of knowing how much money has been invested in the place by way of French doors and nickel-plated ceiling fans and cabinets purposely designed to look old and worn, but everyone knows that by now. These days I loathe Zillow, but back in 2006 I kind of liked it because it suggested my house was worth more than what I'd paid for it.

What I hated about Zillow, though, was that it told me stuff about my neighbors that, despite my natural nosiness, I really didn't want to know. Namely, it told me what they paid for their houses, which, if they'd bought before 2004, was usually much, much less than what I'd paid. I resented having this information because it sent me back to my envy-laced days in New York, where apartments were measured not by what you did with 'them or even in them but by how little you paid in comparison to what they were worth. This was an awful feeling, but still, I couldn't stop Zillowing people, especially those older and more established than I was. I looked up the houses of my editors at the *L.A. Times,* of the local politician who lived around the corner, of a tiny handful of celebrities whose addresses I happened to know. This was an absurd waste of time, but I was not the only person doing it. A wealthy, ostensibly extremely busy woman with whom I had brief professional dealings admitted to also doing it. When we met for the first and only time, we made small talk for a few minutes until she let it slip that she knew what neighborhood I lived in.

"How did you know that?" I asked.

"I Zillowed you," she said without apology. Then she made a pouty face, the kind of face a mean girl in junior high might make while pointing out that the price tag was still on your dress and it said $7.99.

"Good for you, though," she added. "Having your own place."

By 2007, even the schadenfreudeic aspects of the home valuation game were starting to be less fun. The credit crisis was revving up its engines and preparing for takeoff. Foreclosures dotted the landscape. According to Zillow, my house was now worth just *slightly* more than what I'd paid for it. The next year, it would be worth exactly what I'd paid for it, and the year after that it would be worth considerably less.

Of course, these were not my botherations or vexations, not the problems of a responsible thirty-year fixed-mortgage holder like myself. To soothe myself, I kept rationalizations in my pockets like Life Savers. I also tried my best only to have real-estate-related conversations with people who also owned and were therefore in the same leaky boat. The world, of course, has always in many ways been divided between renters and owners, between those who've committed and those who haven't, between those who care what shape their foundation is in and those who don't. But by 2007, that divide had new and different contours; the tables were rapidly turning. Renters regarded owners—at least those of more recent vintage—as cautionary tales. Owners saw renters as smug beneficiaries of their own childishness and risk adversity. Thus, many discussions about our houses and their attendant mortgages tended to devolve into desperate, self-directed pep talks. Hence the following statements, many of which I have repeated no fewer than two hundred times between 2007 and the present day.

"So maybe buying in 2004 wasn't a great idea, but we all do things on our own timetables. Nothing could have stopped me—and at least I didn't buy in 2006."

"At least I'm not upside down." (My loan is not in excess of what the house is worth.)

"It's not like I was a short-term investor. The plan was to stay on Escalada Terrace forever, or at least for a long, long time. Maybe even forever. By the time I'm eighty, surely the house will have appreciated."

The reason homeowners should only say these things to fellow homeowners is that the fellow owners will respond appropriately, which, in a word, is this: "Totally." (As in, "You're totally not a short-term investor; you're totally not upside down; you totally did the right thing in buying your house.")

Say these things to a renter and he is apt to tell you a "really crazy story" about how he approached the landlord about lowering the rent because of the tough economic times and the landlord "totally said yes! How crazy is that?"

To my surprise as well as to his, Alan and I were still together six months after we met in the *L.A. Times* lobby. Before we knew it, we'd been together for twelve months, then sixteen. Unlike some of my past relationships, which sometimes seemed more like performances than relationships, Alan and I were managing to coexist without artifice. We did things for each other. He came up with column ideas for me and looked after Rex when I went out of town (he developed a gushing, jubilant love for Rex). I helped him train for the Boston Marathon by sleeping for six weeks in an oxygen-deprivation tent he'd installed over his bed that was designed to improve lung capacity. I'm laughing as I type this. Sleeping in an oxygen-deprivation tent is the kind of thing you (at least I) only do at the beginning of a relationship. Six months later, I would have said, "I'll see you when your experiment's over." Today I wouldn't let such an apparatus through the front door. But in the winter of 2007 I did this without complaint, and in the spring of 2007 I flew to Boston and watched Alan finish the race in the wind and freezing rain (in three hours and eight minutes; hooray for oxygen deprivation).

But all was not perfect. Consider the following questions, which I found myself pondering at length during this time: When did the definition of "being in a relationship" begin to translate to "always realizing I forgot to pack my other shoe"? Has it been since the late 1960s (or whenever the sexual revolution supposedly began, which no one ever seems to agree on) that adult couples who are "going steady" have seen their lives reduced to commutes between apartments? How come the wedding announcements in *The New York Times* never state what has to be the truth at least 40 percent of the time, that "the couple, who met at the Shark Bar on Amsterdam Avenue, dated for two years until they decided to marry because the lack of counter space in each other's bathrooms caused contact lens cases to fall in toilets one too many times"? How come no term has been coined for the particular feeling of dishevelment that results from going directly to work from your boyfriend/girlfriend's house, a rumpled outfit (hastily chosen and incompletely assembled the evening before) accompanying rumpled tresses (naturally you forgot your hair product) and a nagging anxiety that, back at home, your freezer door has been slightly ajar for twenty-four hours?

I'm inventing the term right now: "nohabitation." The precursor to cohabitation (and, in fairness, also to breaking up), it's what causes a lot of couples to abandon their efforts at maintaining separate quarters—and the autonomy, self-respect, and "healthy boundaries" supposedly entailed therein—and join households. Sometimes, of course, marriage is officially on the horizon. And sometimes one person loses a job, and the couple can no longer afford two rents. But almost as often, I've noticed, permanent commitment has been merely hinted at rather than discussed out loud. In couples past the roommates/entry-level-job/futon-on-the-floor stage, this can be pretty heedless. After all, decent apartments and maybe even biological clocks are ostensibly in the mix. But when the alternative is nohabitation, a broken lease and a lost security deposit are sometimes small prices to pay. That's because despite sounding like a misnomer, despite the ways in which you might think a better term would be "bi-habitation," nohabitation actually plays out very much as it sounds. After a year or more, that exhausting volley between "my place or yours" becomes a tyranny. You may think you're living in two places, but you're actually living nowhere.

Alan and I nohabitated for a year and a half. Though I felt my house to be infinitely more comfortable and inviting than his apartment, I tried to be fair and spend as much time at his place as he did at mine. But as though the house were a living thing capable of feeling abandoned, I hated being away from it. I felt nervous, even guilty about leaving it alone overnight. In some of my sillier—which is not to say disingenuous— moments, I imagined the house springing to mischievous life while I was away. I imagined the cracked floor joists and rusted plumbing parts ruthlessly mocking me for being in such denial about their existence. I imagined the curtains anthropomorphizing into lissome goblins that would open the cupboards and steal the cereal.

Alan, by his own admission—maybe even as a point of pride—had certain challenges in the commitment department. He wasn't comfortable referring to me as his "girlfriend" until after we'd been together at least four months. He also had a habit of saying things like "I'd like to move to China/ I want a cabin in Montana/Why not buy a house in Pasadena?/ I'd definitely go on a years-long space mission if given the opportunity" within the same three-minute span of time. In retrospect, I can see that I was actually comforted by this. Not one to lose at my own game, I unfurled the flag of my own neuroses and hoisted it up even higher. "I'm buying a farm in Nebraska within the next six years," I'd say. Other favorite topics included my desire to spend at least three months of every year at an artists' colony (until I could get my own up and running on the Nebraska farm), my vow never, *ever* to sacrifice things like charm and original woodwork for things like safe neighborhoods and good school districts, and, above all, my

unyielding belief that my house was a one-person house—
make that a one-person-plus-one-dog house—and that making
it into a two-person house would be a very bad idea.

But after fourteen months of nohabitation, we began to
alternate between these topics and the topic of moving in
together. It was wasteful, after all, for him to pay rent while I
was making a mortgage payment every month. It was a bit
ridiculous to be getting five daily newspapers between us and
paying two sets of utility bills and letting too much produce
spoil in the fridge because we hadn't gotten around to using it
in time. Still, I believe we were both somewhat surprised by
the emergence of this issue. Not in an uncharted-waters kind
of way, but in a déjà vu–ish kind of way. We'd both lived with
people before (and it didn't escape my notice that the house
I'd shared with Ex in Nebraska was just as small as the house
on Escalada Terrace). We'd both expressed that these cohabi-
tations had been good, useful, decidedly nonregrettable experiences but that if we were to do it again, it would not be
without a relatively sincere intention to marry the fellow
cohabitant.

"I wouldn't move in with someone again unless the wedding
was already being planned," Alan said one evening in late 2006.
We were half sitting, half lying on my living room sofa, which
was entirely too short for him, reading two separate copies of
the same *New York Times*.

"Oh God, me neither," I said. "And even then, I don't know.
Don't some married people live separately?"

He might have thought I was kidding, but I wasn't.

Still, by the summer of 2007 we were surveying the rooms
and closets of my house, wondering if there was space for
Alan's books and wetsuits and surfboards among my books and
gazillion file folders and all those unfortunate, oversized Soft

Surroundings clothes. None of this, of course, was because we were one "save the date" card away from matrimony. It was because, despite living just slightly more than three miles from each other, we were buckling under the strain of nohabitation. I was sick of the perpetual tower of dirty dishes in his sink; he was sick of there being no room in my closets for his work clothes.

But such headaches were nothing compared with what had arguably become the biggest problem in our relationship: the fact that it was often nearly impossible to park on Alan's street. So crammed was his block with multiple-family houses and apartment buildings whose parking facilities were totally incommensurate to the number of people apparently living in them that I often wondered if I should just start walking the three miles (unthinkable in L.A.). To go to his place after 6:00 p.m. was to join a caravan of anxious, slow-moving vehicles cruising for empty spaces. Oftentimes, cars would just sit there—radio blasting or the driver reclining back and talking on his cell phone—until a pedestrian appeared on the sidewalk, at which point that pedestrian would be followed to his car and the space immediately seized. Other times, large SUVs could be seen attempting to shoehorn themselves into spaces that weren't really spaces, their bumpers tapping the surrounding vehicles until car alarms went off and irate owners stormed out of houses threatening to break knees. More than once, when I got frustrated to the point of tears trying to park, I called Alan from my cell and made him take the car and look for a space himself. Once I made an entire dinner of broiled salmon and roasted potatoes in the time it took him to park my car and walk back to his apartment.

And this is why we decided to move in together. Not because we necessarily wanted to get hitched, but because we wanted to be able to park. In the late summer of 2007, we took the first tiny steps toward combining our households. Alan moved his Persian rug into my living room, and I took the white cotton rug that had been in my living room and moved it into the bedroom. When he brought over his Turkish kilim and declared that it should go in the bedroom, I moved the white cotton rug into the kitchen. When it became evident that having a rug in the kitchen caused the table to wobble and made it impossible to pull the chairs out, I put it in a garbage bag with some of my Soft Surroundings purchases and took it to Goodwill.

The guest room, we determined, would be Alan's "personal space." The wrought-iron futon would be his to throw his clothes on; the closet would be entirely under his jurisdiction. So over the course of a four-day weekend during which he was climbing to the top of Mount Whitney with an equally aerobically endowed friend, I emptied the closet. This took four days because it required not just sorting through the random dusty, broken, and often unidentifiable crap I'd thrown in there— winter coats, my graduate school thesis, that same goddamned stereo equipment I'd dragged from dorm to dorm at Vassar and still haven't thrown away because it still works and always seems too "valuable"—but also transferring much of it into the bedroom closet, which in turn demanded its own aggressive weeding out. By the end of the weekend I had seven bags of garbage, five bags of Goodwill items, and a depressing amount of items that could not be thrown away but for which there was no storage room.

And so it went with the cohabitation preparations. I would clear a few things out, Alan would bring a few things in, and, not having room for any of it, we'd cram the stuff in corners until the house attained a certain *Grey Gardens*–like ataxia. He put one bicycle and the box of rock-climbing gear in the back room. We argued over the TV. Mine was too small, and his was too bulky. His would protrude too much in the living room, I insisted. Besides (ever my mother's daughter), I couldn't stand the thought of having a TV in the living room for all to see. The TV, of course, was best hidden out of sight in the guest room, hence the wrought-iron futon, hence the absence of Victorian dollhouse wallpaper (not that he'd witnessed that particular atrocity), but now that he'd be occupying the guest room, we had no choice but to become middlebrow people with a TV in the living room.

We talked about money, about how much he'd pay in rent and how much I already paid in mortgage and whether or not he'd kick in for the cleaning lady and the gardener (yes) and the property tax and insurance (no). He asked why my monthly nut appeared to be far less than my actual monthly expenses, and when I'd say I didn't know (although hard salami from Whole Foods can be expensive), he'd get confused and huffy and I'd get defensive and self-loathing and start worrying that I'd never again be allowed to make a dinner of salami and wine and eat it while staring at the wall listening to some female singer-songwriter warble about choosing independence over love.

My friends, who approved of our relationship far more enthusiastically than they had any of my past ones, mostly told me to sally forth, to work it out, to not let a good guy fall away because of anxieties over salami. A few looked me straight in the eye and said, "He'll never marry you if you let him move in; your name from now on will be Free Milk. There will be no purchasing of cows." I found this troubling, though perhaps not quite as much as I found it ever so slightly relieving. Still, most people insisted it was absolutely the right thing, that the house was plenty big for both of us—after living in New York, how could I possibly see a freestanding house as too small?— that I was plenty old enough to make the right decision. Someone even suggested to me that cohabitation was a "greener" lifestyle choice than the apparently planet-raping scourges of nohabitation. Granted, my father worried out loud that I was giving up my freedom and my solitude, that this surrender to bourgeois convention could bite me in the ass in any number of life-busting ways. "What if he wants to watch TV while you want to read?" he asked, genuine panic rising in his voice. My mother, however, was charmed by Alan and elated that I'd found someone with health insurance (even though I wouldn't be partaking of it). She offered to buy us a flat-screen TV if we moved in together. I'm not sure she caught the part about it being in the living room.

So we agreed to a fresh start on the TV front. Alan sold his to a friend, and I donated mine, which was five years old and now apparently worth less than a package of batteries, to Goodwill. Too proud to remind my mother about her offer, we purchased our own high-definition flat screen for $800, only to discover that the high-def signal only worked about half the time.

Then came the sofa discussion. My sofa, an elegant gray love seat I'd purchased when I moved into the Silver Lake house, was too short for the six-foot three-inch Alan. When he lay on it, everything from his knees down hung off the edge. His sofa, on the other hand, was long and large and bursting with overstuffed cushions and would have been entirely out of proportion with my living room. But he adored this sofa. Somehow he loved it as if it were a pet, as if it were his own giant, inanimate version of Rex. But these affections, to me, were beside the point. There was, for starters, the problem of the untenable layout of the room. As much as we squabbled over the benefits and limitations of our particular sofas, the fact was that the positions of the front door, the windows, the faux fireplace, and the heat register really allowed no place for any sofa. This was a living room that cried out for beanbag chairs or Japanese-style mats, not real furniture. The sofa I already had barely worked as it was. Perhaps, I suggested, we should have no sofa at all. And maybe we should return the TV while we were at it.

Alan is a problem solver. His almost compulsive need to find solutions darted around our conversations until we were not so much decorating as working a Rubik's Cube that had suddenly disguised itself as a house. We moved shelves, rotated the rug, and reconfigured chairs. We bought used credenzas from Craigslist and new credenzas from IKEA and stuffed them with electronics equipment and extra blankets and dog toys and anything bereft of a rightful place, which in this house was just about everything except the stove.

On the fourth week of sofa talks, Alan arrived at the answer.

"I will saw my sofa in half," he said.

He measured the wall and the doorway (of course he measured the doorway). Then he went home and measured his sofa and declared that it would fit in my house if it was one-third shorter than its current length. Then he went on the Internet and Googled "furniture alteration" and (true) "sofa shortening." And when I said I would not let his sofa in my house at any length because it was (a) no longer its original off-white color but rather, thanks to food stains and sweat stains and a million newspapers piled on it at all times, something a catalog might describe as "darkened dishwater" and (b) far too gargantuan in width and depth for a reduction of length to make any difference whatsoever, Alan told me not to be so closed minded and insensitive. I then told him not to be so completely retarded. I told him that his sofa, even if operated on by some mythical maestro of sofa surgeons and transformed into a seamless, scar-free, shorter version of itself, would look stupid and terrible and ruin *everything*. I was not being closed minded, I said, but speaking from experience, from painful, putrid, candle- and dog-shit-scented experience (and here my voice was rising in panic as I recalled the shadow cast by the media cabinet in Dani's cottage in Venice), and that this experience taught me that there was *nothing* worse than having furniture that's too big for your house. Not even your house catching on fire was worse. Not even falling asleep on the beach and having ants crawl in your nose and into your brain would be worse. And because this sofa was the first real piece of furniture Alan had ever bought, because he'd had it custom made when he'd lived in New York and had his first real job, and because he'd then shipped it to Mexico City and then later to L.A., and because the sofa had cost him $2,750, which he could prove to me because he still had the receipt because unlike me he kept all his receipts, because unlike me he knew the value of things and didn't just want to replace everything all the time, Alan became enraged and I became enraged and the evening dissolved into an echo chamber of accusations and denials and, in odd moments, valid points. I noted that he still hadn't given his landlord a thirty-day moving-out notice. He pointed out that aside from emptying the guest room closet, I had done nothing to make him feel "welcome" in my home. And, incidentally, he hated the futon. Always had. The feel of velvet against his skin repelled him, he said. (Ditto for velour and suede; I should know this about him.)

The next morning we decided—calmly and without a trace

of anger or blame—that we wouldn't move in together just yet. We would wait until we'd been a couple for longer (like, say, three years) and had a more solid commitment and could possibly buy a bigger house. I said I thought that was an excellent idea. I reiterated that the house really was a one-person house. I mean, look at it! I said. No garage, no basement, only three tiny closets, and one of them contains the washer and dryer and water heater and filing cabinet and office supplies and CDs. Where would his stuff go? Alan was by now a competitive road cyclist. He had three bikes, all of which were very expensive and handcrafted and couldn't have been kept in a garage or basement even if I'd had a garage or a basement. No fair to those bikes! I said. Let's wait!

"I feel really good about this," I said.

"Me too," he said.

That night, Alan drove home to his apartment after work and spent one hour and five minutes looking for a parking space. He moved into my house a month later.

He moved in, but not before I'd investigated other options. In the quest to find a workable transition from nohabitation to cohabitation, no stone was unturned, no scenario unimagined, no Internet photo unclicked. Whereas in most areas of life (such as exercise or cooking . . . any other area of life really) procrastination is my default setting, I'm happy to drop everything and do what needs to be done when real estate is the issue or problem at hand. And amid this quandary, it crossed my mind that renting might be the thing that needed to be done.

"If I could get, say, $2,100 in rent for this house," I posited out loud, "that would leave us free to rent something way nicer and bigger for, say, $3,500. Which means we'd each be paying

$1,750, which is less than my mortgage now, which means I'd have enough left over to pay property taxes and repairs and everything else."

"But you still have to pay your monthly mortgage, which is $2,054," said Mr. Show-Off Math Genius. "You're getting rent money but it has to go to the mortgage."

"Oh . . . right."

Again, let's understand something about addiction. It can go dormant, it can retract back underneath its shell, but it's always just below the surface. It's always waiting for a trigger. In my case, all I need is for someone to say, "I read that Whoozitville is the hot, up-and-coming neighborhood these days," and, before I know it, I'm upended again. And that is what started to happen. I needed a fix. As ultimately uninterested as I was at that point in moving out of the house on Escalada Terrace and as much as I couldn't stand the thought of another year of nohabitation, the notion of having to share my place with someone—even someone as beloved as Alan— knocked me sufficiently off course that I returned to my old habits. I went back on realtor.com and Craigslist and the MLS Web site. I pictured us in a sprawling mid-century modern with a workroom for his bikes and a separate office for me. I pictured us in a voluptuous Craftsman reading our individual newspapers in front of a stone fireplace. Mostly, I just pictured us someplace bigger, someplace with closets, someplace not quite so steeped in the colic of my efforts at self-definition. In other words, someplace *ours*.

And so my loyalty to Escalada Terrace was tested. As had been the case during my previous tour of real estate voyeurism/ enslavement, it wasn't just the possibility—however remote— of the "perfect" house that ignited my cravings. It was the reminder that one's own house wasn't the only house in the world, that pledging yourself to one piece of property doesn't mean you'll never know the embrace of another. This, of course, was the reasoning that had allowed me to buy the house, despite my lack of total infatuation with it, in the first place. And now, clicking through duplexes and bungalows and (when I got bored of the L.A. listings and expanded my reach across Topanga and Malibu and up the coast all the way to Oregon) A-frames and cabins and yurts, the manic birr of those old shopping days returned. I wanted to live on another block, in another part of town, in New York, in Paris, on the moon. Some of these places I wanted to inhabit with Alan ("journalist couple relocates to space station; follow them on Twitter"), while others cried out for a cloistered, possibly chain-smoking existence in a rented attic with a stove-top espresso maker and a view of the Seine.

As before, this form of virtual window-shopping was exhausting, even frightening. Like a man taken to a strip club the night before his wedding, I experienced the houses as both objects of terror and objects of salvation. Lotharios made of wood and stone and Tyvek weatherizing wrap, the houses conjured a furious, emotional seesaw of possibilities and improbabilities and visions of lives unlived, roads untaken, lawns unmowed, rooms uninhabited—at least by me.

But what about spaces undeveloped? There was always the garage, of course. I hadn't forgotten my grand guesthouse plan. It was a long-range plan, a plan I had no designs on implementing unless I happened to find $80,000 hidden inside the crawl space above my bedroom closet. But maybe it wouldn't be that much, I now thought. Or maybe I could take out a loan. Maybe I could build the guesthouse, and Alan could keep his stuff in it—or even kind of live in it on days when we were tired of each other. At the very least, maybe he could keep his bicycles in the garage; it would, after all, be no ordinary garage but state-of-the-art.

I called a contractor. I took him through the upper yard, into the lower yard, and down the stairs. I told him the bones of the garage were there but it just needed a little updating.

"Minimum $100,000," he said. "I've rarely seen such a disaster. You need an engineer. You need soil reports. You need an architect. You need several months of construction."

"What if it was just the garage but not the guesthouse?" I asked.

"What guesthouse?" he asked.

I called another contractor.

"Minimum $200,000," he said.

I don't know why, but I called yet another one. The rule of thumb with estimates is that you get three and take the middle one. Somehow I felt compelled to do this, even though I wasn't going to be embarking on this project anytime in the current millennium.

"Two hundred and seventy-five thousand dollars," said the third contractor. "And by the way, the retaining wall next to your house is unsafe and not up to code. I'd recommend doing that first. Probably for around $60,000."

Maybe I should sell the house, I thought. Not that I wanted to, not really, not at all. But one weekend, when Alan was out of town with two of his three bikes competing in a race that required him to ride insane distances at insane elevations, I sat at my desk eating my salami and realized how much I missed him. I was terrified of letting him move in, but, I now realized, I was also terrified of him not moving in. Moreover, I wanted him to move in not just for parking-related reasons but because—and, as revelations go, this was so simple as to be embarrassing—I wanted to be near him. If not constantly, at least more often than not. Why was I clinging to my house as if it were the only thing that made me worthy of love? Why was I lording over it so zealously, stopping people at the door as though I were some numskull nightclub bouncer? Why was I holding it out in front of me like a shield?

Maybe I should sell the house, I thought. Maybe I should just free myself from it—even at no profit—and rent a whole new place with Alan. Not only would a rental be a clean slate, a neutral space in which our lives could commingle without the baggage of someone's life already having been there, but it would undoubtedly be larger and nicer than what we were currently working with. That was the solution, I decided. I would join Alan among the ranks of the smug renters. If things didn't work out, at least I would have sold my house before the market got *really* bad (and this was coming; every five minutes on CNBC they were announcing that the housing apocalypse was nigh). If things did work out, maybe we'd buy a new house in a year or two.

I called Michael, the Realtor. He was happy I finally had a boyfriend. He said he'd come over and tell me what I needed to do with my house if I wanted to sell it. It was now August 2007. Zillow believed my house was worth no more than $503,000. Michael didn't try to influence me one way or the other, but he did say that if I was worried about the market that year, I'd be considerably more worried the following year. He also said that in order to make it "attractive" to potential buyers, I'd need to do the following:

- Replace the windows in the kitchen, living room, and bedroom

- Repaint the entire back room, as the white was looking "dirty"

- Repaint the bedroom, as the mint green was "a bit of a personal choice"

- Replace the doorknobs so that they don't fall off in your hand

- Lay down fresh sod in the backyard because the grass is brown from the dog peeing on it

- Define the back room as either an office, a dining room, an exercise room, or a laundry room but not all four at once, because that can confuse the buyer and give him or her an unconscious perception of disorder

- Redo the kitchen cabinets, which look a little "shabbier" than "chic"

- Install mirror in faux fireplace and assemble candles on the floor; gives a chic and festive look and creates the illusion of a working fireplace (idea I saw on *Trading Spaces*: optional)

Michael did, however, like the yellow walls in the kitchen.

I decided not to sell the house. Instead, for the next week, I reverted to my plan of renting it out and then moving with Alan into another, bigger rental. I tried to get my math straight this time. If we could find something for $2,500 a month, we could swing it. But considering I was hoping to rent my own house for that amount, how did I expect to find something bigger and better for the same? Maybe we could venture into an "up and coming" neighborhood, I thought. Maybe I was being too pessimistic about the potential rent value of my house. Maybe someone would come along who absolutely loved blue walls and distressed wood cabinets and was willing to pay above market for them. Maybe I'd be walking Rex in the park one day and happen upon an old carriage house. Maybe the caretaker would emerge from the house at the precise moment I was passing by and hang up a For Rent sign. Maybe the care-taker would explain to me that the house was very special, that he'd lived there for years but could no longer manage the stairs. Maybe he'd tell me that the rent was normally $3,000 but given that I had such a nice dog and seemed like such a nice person—such a *deserving* person—he'd rent it to me for $1,500.

I mentioned none of these machinations to Alan.

What lay at the root of the addiction into which I'd relapsed? How had I managed to take my supreme good fortune (and, based on my track record, finding the love of a good, smart, sane man was nothing if not stupendously supreme good for-tune) and convert it into a housing crisis? At the time, I would have said it was all a matter of not having enough space, of there being insufficient room for the sofa, the TV, the bikes. But now I know it was plain fear: fear of entrapment, of becoming needy, of cutting off my options. One of the chief lessons of growing up of course is recognizing that choosing one path usually necessitates forgoing another. And while even back then I was generally able to cope with the numerous opportunities that were no longer available to me—a career as a neurosurgeon, musical prodigy–hood, being a virgin bride—somehow real estate remained a vessel of hope. As long as there was a new house on the horizon, I had a shot at redemp-tion, transformation, or at least new and better paint colors. If

I could live everywhere, I reasoned unreasonably, maybe I could live forever.

And as drawn as I was to the idea of buying real estate, the rush was often more intense when it came to rentals. It doesn't take a genius to see why. A rental is the housing equivalent of, if not a one-night stand, the kind of relationship where introductions are made to friends but not to parents. It's a B-plus kind of situation, comfortably adequate, maybe even all the better for its distance from any possibility of perfection. To live in a rental is to wake up every morning believing that your life hasn't started yet. It is to spend months or years or even decades nursing the belief that things are going to get better, that the Big Trade-Up is yet to come. As much as I wanted to actually purchase real estate, as many Sunday afternoons as I spent skulking around open houses, nothing remained as (theoretically) intoxicating as the possibility of trying out a new rental. The notion of a new neighborhood with its attendant new supermarket and new dry cleaner and new route to the airport is as enticing as a good kiss after a mediocre date. It was all about possibility without commitment, fresh starts that would invariably end.

On the other hand, I had a good career, a good man, and a good house. The dramatic posturing around indecision and "loving my freedom" was wearing thin. It was time to grow up. Besides, I loved the house on Escalada Terrace. I loved the palm tree in the front yard and the patio table in the backyard and the hill across the street and the coyotes that sauntered around driveways in broad daylight. Why not share it with someone? My house, after all, was as much a piece of my metaphorical heart as were the actual pieces of my actual heart. What was the big deal about keeping a couple of bicycles and some rock-climbing gear in the back room near my desk?

I took a photo of the wrought-iron futon and put it on Craigslist, describing it as "a truly unique piece" and asking $200. A week later, when no one bit, I lowered the price to $175. A week later, $100. Two different people wrote and said they'd buy it for $75. I told them to come right over, but they never did. Three days before Alan had to be out of his apartment, I modified the ad to say I'd give the futon away for free to whoever came and got it in the next forty-eight hours. When the forty-eight hours passed, I asked Marta, the cleaning lady, if she wanted it or knew of anyone who might. She did not. Then I offered it to Fernando, the gardener. Despite being from Mexico, Fernando had a voice and an accent that made him a dead ringer for that old *Saturday Night Live* character, the Italian priest Father Guido Sarducci.

I showed him the futon. I explained that it was difficult to get through the door but that it could be done. I told him it was a nice, unique piece.

"I do not a'want it," Fernando said.

"Really?" I said, recalling, almost mortifyingly, the toil—once seemingly Herculean, now clearly fatuous—of getting it through the door not even two years earlier.

"But maybe I can find someone who does."

Fernando went outside and got his assistant, who was clearing bougainvillea petals off the patio with a leaf blower. They came back in and, with great difficulty and a very near miss with the Restoration Hardware pendant light fixture on the kitchen ceiling, moved the futon frame into the front yard.

"I will come a'later today with the bigger truck," Fernando said. "I have'a an idea of where to take it."

He did not come later that day or the next day or the next day. The futon sat in the yard like an iron sculpture on some kind of hippie commune. Meanwhile, the purple velvet cushion sat on the floor of the otherwise empty guest room. Along with the naked lightbulb hanging from the ceiling fan, you'd have thought it was a room in a Thai brothel—or the backdrop in an American Apparel ad.

Finally, on the third day, Fernando came back with the truck.

"Did you find someone who wants it?" I asked. "Because, you know, it's a nice . . . uh, piece."

"Don't a'worry, I'll take it," Fernando said. He smiled as if he felt sorry for me. He smiled as if he pitied me for having such bad judgment and bad taste. And together we lifted the frame into the truck, and then we dragged the mattress outside, the sidewalk scraping grooves into the velvet, the grass burrowing into those grooves. It was clear the futon was going to no one. It was clear it was headed to Goodwill, if not the dump. Fernando got into his truck and drove down the hill. I watched the futon bouncing in the truck bed as it faded into the distance, first five feet, then ten feet, then the distance of the whole street and around the corner, and then gone forever. And in that moment I promised myself that this would be the last futon of my life. I promised myself that I would sooner sleep on the floor or never again host an overnight guest than resort to buying another futon. From that point on I would be a grown-up. Or at least sleep like one.

And I did. Alan had an expensive Tempur-Pedic mattress and a crummy bed, and I had my expensive, handmade cherrywood bed and a crummy mattress. Harmony, for once. We moved his mattress into the bedroom and dragged mine out to the yard. I called the sanitation department to come and get it. In the twenty-four hours between the time that the mattress was placed in the yard and when it was collected by the sanitation department's bulky-item curbside collection service, a

Google Earth satellite photo was taken of the house, capturing the mattress in perfect detail. For the next several years, the photo associated with just about every Internet image of my house would show a mattress in the yard.

When I think back on the period during which Alan was moving into my house, I see it as a three-month version of trying to get that wrought-iron futon through the guest room door. Though as a former New Yorker I still find it obscene to complain about lack of space when one lives in a bona fide house with an upper and a lower yard, it is difficult to overstate the degree to which our joining of households resembled the stuffing of two dozen clowns into a Yugo. And as much as I'd like to say that we eventually pulled it together and pruned the place down into a clean, well-lit sanctuary, the truth is that we didn't and haven't. The process of learning how to live with each other was really a process of learning how to live with each other's stuff and, when necessary, discarding it in favor of new stuff.

That said, we were not people in possession of a tremendous amount of stuff. I was not the woman with forty bottles of face cream on the bathroom counter and sixty pairs of shoes organized by color in the closet. He was not the guy with a sprawling, table-mounted electric train set or a sports car that required its own heated garage. As a longtime home-office worker, I did have an enormous amount of folders and ink cartridges and jumbo packs of Post-its and errant papers that I was perpetually unable to either file away or discard. (I'll also admit to a minor obsession with handmade gift wrapping paper, which I kept, along with assorted ribbons and cards and colored tissue paper, in an enormous, perpetually overflowing shopping bag in the office supply/washer dryer/water heater closet.) As a resolute and sometimes fanatical athlete, Alan did have more sports equipment than I ever imagined would be found under my roof. But in the relative scheme of things, we were more ascetic than acquisitional. We had one TV, one window air conditioner, one bathroom, and essentially one bedroom. We tried not to bring a new book in the house without finding a way to gently dispose of an old one. When I got Alan a giant exercise ball for his birthday, we incorporated it into the seating.

The way we broke through the impasse regarding the sofa was this: First, Alan sold his beloved sofa to the neighbors across the street. "That way I can go visit it," he said. "It's not like I've totally given it up." Second, we purchased (from IKEA, naturally) a dark leather chaise called the Kramfors. The idea was that it was sufficiently low-slung so as not to overpower the room and also that it could be placed several inches away from the wall, thereby avoiding the heat register. Backless, armless, and not even four feet long, it was straight out of a psychoanalyst's office as depicted in a *New Yorker* cartoon. It was also about as comfortable as a bench seat in an old station wagon. Both of us could sit on it if we were willing to sit up straight, but it was impossible for two people to lie on it at the same time. Whenever Rex climbed up and tried to stretch out on the thing, he often slid off and landed on the heat register. Buying this chaise was not the most brilliant stroke, though the thing did at least look nice.

Much else about the house did not look as nice. Almost every surface of every shelf and table and counter was covered with bills or receipts or magazines or plastic drink bottles for Alan's bikes or vitamin bottles or clothing catalogs. Every bookshelf was double stacked, every closet packed floor to ceiling, every inch of cabinet space jammed so tightly with

boxes of cereal, pasta, and vacuum-sealed soup that you had to
pry items out using your entire arm, which often caused the
shelf to wobble and knock everything onto the counter or even
the floor. If any piece of furniture had space underneath it,
we'd shove stuff into that space. Folded-up rugs and plastic
garbage bags containing bulky comforters and extra pillows
collected dust beneath the bed. Bicycle tools and boxes of
Alan's files and receipts—those treasured receipts!—were
shoved underneath the dining table. Under my desk lay a huge
plastic container shipped to me by my mother when she
moved out of New Jersey and into Manhattan, and its contents were veritable advertisements for stuff you don't know
what to do with if you have no storage: Christmas ornaments,
high-school yearbooks, junior-high-school report cards, programs from various concerts and recitals, a tenth-grade English
paper on *The Rise of Silas Lapham* on which I'd received an A
minus. At any given time, piles of laundry sat on the dining
table, which we used for eating a handful of times in the first
year, then gave up on altogether.

The guest room was no longer called a guest room, as it no
longer housed a guest. But given its inexorable dismalness, I
imagine that Alan sometimes wished he were. In the beginning, thinking he'd get a desk for it, we made several trips to
IKEA and debated the merits of the Johan versus the Vika
Amon versus the Expedit. Abandoning the desk idea, he
decided to get an imitation Eames chair called the Poäng, in
which he planned to recline with his laptop and do important
work while I was doing my important work at my desk in the
back room. As it turned out, Alan would do this approximately
two times before the chair became the official repository for
clothes for which there was no drawer or closet space.

Still, it was a nice chair, if an utterly commonplace one in the post-IKEA world—the neighbors came over and said, "Oh, the Poäng!"—and something about having it in the house was gratifying despite its being barely recognizable beneath the clothes. The lines were clean and minimal, the exact inverse of the house itself. And the few times Alan sat in it, reading *The Economist* under the framed photographs of Rwandan prisoners that he'd hung on the wall to make the place feel like his own, I'd imagine him as an older man, a man with gray hair and knobby hands and reading glasses exercising his God-given right to sit in his reclining chair. And then I'd hope to God we wouldn't still be living on Escalada Terrace when we got to be that old.

One Sunday afternoon in the spring of 2008, I dragged Alan to an open house in a nearby historic neighborhood. He wasn't usually keen to make these excursions, but since I had so few other hobbies, he tolerated them the way someone might tolerate a partner's ceramic-figurine collection. We stepped inside the house, and it was a knockout. Jaw-dropping, mind-numbing, totally our thing (our names might as well have been spray painted across the front, albeit in very expensive paint). A perfectly preserved Craftsman with a massive stone fireplace, four bedrooms, a finished attic, and (magically, almost Narnia-like) *two* staircases, the house seemed to go on forever; it was an extra-room dream that wasn't a dream. The price was $889,999. This number was staggeringly high, but since at least it wasn't $1 million, we allowed ourselves to stay and talk with the Realtor for nearly an hour. We talked about the house for days afterward. We wondered how much the seller would come down on the price (it was, after all, 2008). The house had its own personal Web site, and we went to it and ogled the photos and sent the link to friends. For a few days, we shared something precious: the dream of space—not just adequate space, but excessive space. In my mind, I moved us into the house. I decorated it. I decided which of those four bedrooms would be my office and which would be a proper guest room. I thought of the people who would come to stay. I imagined my mother walking through the door and saying, "Meghan, this is your house!"

Of course, we didn't buy it. For a million reasons we didn't even seriously consider buying it. For one thing, it was $889,999. For another, despite its interior splendors, its outdoor features were seriously lacking. There was almost no yard, it was surrounded by apartment buildings, and the neighborhood, while "historic," was known for its crime problems. There was also the minor, mostly unspoken issue of our commitment level. Though our cohabitation had eased into an amicable, affectionate, and apparently sustainable lifestyle, we rarely talked of marriage. This was partly because we were genuinely afraid to and partly because, since neither of us was particularly gung ho about having kids, we didn't really need to.

Some of our paralysis, though, also came from being crammed into a tiny house that we really could not leave. The clutter and crowdedness made us angry at each other, which in turn made us question our compatibility, which in turn made us not want to take steps toward a formal commitment. When I suggested this to a psychoanalyst I know, she suggested the problem might have metaphorical, "unconscious" dimensions. She thought the crowding I felt was emotional rather than literally spatial. She thought my desire for a bigger house was actually a desire for more space in the relationship. Normally, I was game for this kind of analysis, but in this instance she was dead wrong. It wasn't as interesting as that. The cigar was just a cigar. The problems with our relationship could be measured in square footage, not unmet childhood needs.

"I invite you to come see the house for yourself," I said. "You will see what I mean. Dr. Freud himself wouldn't try to get Freudian with this one."

Occasionally I'd see houses for sale that were ridiculous. I'd see oddly shaped bungalows or Gothic, dilapidated Victorians or shacks that had been embellished with enough bohemian details—a cow's skull over the doorway, a toilet turned into a flowerpot in the yard—to momentarily trick me into finding some kind of appeal in them. Always, I'd think that these were the sorts of houses I'd look at and seriously think about purchasing if I was still single. These were the sorts of places— like farms in Nebraska and lonely one-room apartments on mountaintops—that made me feel like the rustic, bohemian girl I have apparently not turned out to be. They were the sorts of places that would unquestionably be a disaster if I actually bought them, though that didn't stop me, during the first few years living with Alan, from playing the whole scenario out in my mind.

One such place was a cabin nestled into an unpaved, largely unknown nearby street that angles off a larger street and curls around into the park. It was essentially a hovel, but the fact that it was painted red and that the online photos showed an easel and a half-finished canvas sitting outside the door made me think it was an artist's paradise. The inside photos showed it to be essentially one big, warehouselike room with a hole cut into the ceiling into which a spiral staircase led to an attic "bedroom." The kitchen, as it were, was a wall of counter space with just enough room for a refrigerator and a stove on either side. The bathroom looked like something the owner installed with his stoned buddies over a weekend. It was not a house but the kind of place you stumble into and sleep in when you're lost in the woods. It was $346,000. There was absolutely no doubt in my mind that if I were single and still house hunting, I would try to buy this place.

For several months, I couldn't get the cabin out of my mind. It's not that I wanted it exactly. It was more that I wanted to eventually be reincarnated as the kind of person who would live and thrive in it. Thinking about the cabin sometimes made me feel as if I were cheating on Alan, but at the same time, when I looked at him, I knew he was saving me from the indignities of everything I already knew about it. Despite our inability to move forward in certain concrete ways he had a way of taking my hand and at least keeping me from going backward.

My mother wanted me to get a bigger place, preferably with a guesthouse so she could move in. She was joking when she said the guesthouse part, of course, but, as was her tendency in matters of real estate, wanderlust threatened to override logic. Unlike my father, who had remained content in his apartment near the Tudor Hotel for nearly fifteen years and had no plans to move—or so much as rearrange one piece of furniture—my mother continued to have a roaming eye. Never mind that she was living in her best interior design effort yet. Installed now in a spacious apartment near the park on West Eighty-sixth Street, she'd waved her divine wand again. Subtle shades of gray and mauve fell into seamless concert where the ceiling met the walls. Her taste in art had evolved over the years from framed museum posters to original pieces, and she made daring use of her wall space, hanging large paintings in small spaces and letting the air breathe around smaller pieces. She kept an orchid on her kitchen windowsill at all times. Her countertop, now as always, held a row of hand-made pottery mugs (a collection started in Palo Alto) that she'd long refused to keep in the cupboard (she had an enduring policy against keeping any dishes hidden away in cupboards, preferring open hutches or, if necessary, removing the cupboard doors altogether). At her desk, she kept photographs taped to the walls and the adjacent shelves (she was aesthetically opposed to small, freestanding picture frames). They showed me and my brother, her and various friends, even Rex, whom she called her "grand dog." But her screen saver, the image that glowed into life whenever you approached the desk, was a photograph she'd taken of her living room. There were no people in it, just furniture and flowers, artwork and colors: the decorated set of her life.

When she wasn't talking about moving to L.A., she talked about moving to northern California, to Vermont, even back to Austin. It wasn't that she'd soured on her apartment—like everywhere she'd lived, she loved it down to the nub by sheer force of decorating—but she didn't feel it was her last stop. She loved saying "I live in Manhattan," but she missed sitting in the garden. She missed having a car. She loved all those restaurants, but she couldn't exactly afford them. She had friends, but they were often busy with work or with grandchildren—something she was unlikely to get anytime soon. (My brother, who still lived in L.A., was resolutely single, though he'd bought a house.)

In early 2009, at the age of sixty-six, my mother was diagnosed with cancer. It was a rare, incurable cancer, and she was at an advanced stage. She began chemotherapy, though the idea was to slow the disease down, not to make it go away. This was a shock unlike anything our dyspeptic family had ever come up against. Our stiff reunion at the cancer center—the first time I can remember us all being together since that evening on West Seventy-eighth Street when my mother commenced her new life as a New Yorker—creaked under the weight of our awkwardness. We neither touched each other much nor said much. There were no tears. A few of my mother's friends had cried when they heard the news but not us. After meeting with the doctors—if treatment went well, she could have a few years; if not, the prognosis was dire—we all went to lunch and talked about nothing in particular.

What was there to say? It was awful and unfair. It was ghastly. My mother, whose life had been nothing if not a series of carefully conceived and vigorously implemented plans, suddenly found herself robbed of the activity she loved most: thinking about the future. Still, she surfed realtor.com.

"Type in zip code 10965," she said to me over the phone after I'd gone home. "There's an Eichler house. I'm sure it needs work, but I've always wanted one."

She told me she knew it was silly to think about moving at a time like this—like a good Midwesterner, she tended to refer to her cancer as "my situation"—but that looking at real estate, at least photographs of real estate, made her feel better. She clicked through images of houses in Westchester County and on Cape Cod, of fisherman's cottages in Maine, of other apartments in Manhattan. She bought a new sofa from Crate and Barrel and an expensive piece of art. She thought about redoing her kitchen. She wanted marble countertops and a checkerboard floor. If the results of her next CAT scan were promising, she told me, she'd price out these renovations. She was prepared to pay for them herself even though the apartment was a rental.

I flew to New York to be with her when the results came back. When we learned that the chemo was working—for now, anyway—we went directly from the cancer center to

Home Depot. By now, my mother had lost most of her hair and was wearing a wig. Her eyelashes were so thinned out that her eyes watered constantly. Still, she had the kitchen dimensions drawn out in her notepad. She showed them to the man in the countertop department and the woman in the floor department, her tissue perpetually dabbing her face as though she'd won a new kitchen on a game show and couldn't contain her emotion. The total cost including installation: $5,919. She said she would think about it. She was suddenly very tired—two excursions in one day were now usually more than she could do—but that she would seriously consider it.

"I'm not sure I want to die in this apartment," she said to me later. We were sitting on her new sofa. The late afternoon light was pressing angled lines against her mauve wall. "It just doesn't feel like home."

For so long, maybe all my life, I thought only a house could make you whole. I thought I was nothing without an interesting address. I thought I was only as good as my color scheme, my drawer pulls, my floors. I can't say I don't still often have those thoughts. But if there's anything that now separates me from the person who haphazardly signed all those inspection reports back in 2004, it's the knowledge that a house can be as fragile as life itself. You'd think it would be stronger, since it can stand in one spot for centuries while generations of humans run through its rooms, grow up, move out, and eventually die. But a house is an inherently limited entity. It can't do everything, or even most things. It cannot give you a personality. It cannot bring you love. It cannot cure loneliness. It can provide comfort, safety, a sense of pride—that much I know. But after forty years of thinking that my ideal self was waiting for me on the other side of a door I hadn't yet had a chance to open, I'm beginning to see that there's more to life than moving. For instance, just being alive.

My mother's chemo didn't work for long. By mid-September, she was in the hospital, the treatment suspended, the doctors "reevaluating." By early October, she was officially dying. It was a surreal autumn, sweet and awful both, at once a jubilation and a cataclysm. That Labor Day weekend, in a moment of unprecedented optimism, Alan and I had decided to get married (he made a genuine proposal and I replied with a genuine yes; how ordinary we were; more surprising yet, what unforeseen elation lay in such ordinariness!) and within weeks it was obvious that the major gift of this wedding would not be money or dishes or a bread maker but the gift we'd give to my mother. We would give her a wedding. Soon and in New York. Not later in California. We would get married in her presence—"I don't care how long I have to wait for your wedding," she'd always said, "I just want to be there"—and because this required notable concessions to our plans (such as they were), the weird, beautiful, terrible truth was that our marriage, or at least our wedding, was as much a recognition of her impending death (and in turn an homage to her life) as a celebration of our commitment.

I wanted, of course, to get married on the hill on Escalada Terrace. I wanted Rex to be there and our friends and neighbors to be there, and I wanted to wait until April when the grass grew tall and prairielike and the late-afternoon sun washed the city in purple-gold light. But it wasn't to be. For a million reasons it wasn't to be, and I'm still grateful to whatever force rose up from within me and kept me from being inconsolably disappointed, or, odder still, terribly disappointed at all. A few nights before we said our vows, I dreamed that my dress was not the off-white beaded charmeuse I'd purchased in a California vintage boutique but a long red shift with a black cape. In the dream I would look in the mirror and see not a bride but the grim reaper with a bouquet of roses and an updo. I would study my face in this mirror, note that my eyes and mouth were still my own, and tell myself that even though this wasn't the dress I had imagined, even though the dress was shapeless and frightening and *red*, I could have a perfectly fine wedding while wearing it. Later I would wake up and wonder if this was the most literal dream I'd had since the dream of the $127-a-month house behind the iron fence all those years ago.

We decided we'd have a small wedding on December 5, a date that seemed crisp and buoyant, like a Martini glass chilled in the freezer or an icicle on a leaf. But my mother's condition worsened—she wanted to find the perfect venue but couldn't quite summon the energy to leave her apartment; she wanted to contact caterers but couldn't always dial the phone properly—and the date became November 21, then November 14, then November 7. In the end, it was October 25, a lustrous and mild day sandwiched between two rainy and cold ones, a day that came up so fast that we had no rings and Alison had to pick up the dress from the tailor, put it in a garment bag, and hand it off to Alan on his way to the airport, where he caught a red-eye to JFK, took a taxi to my mother's apartment, and went with me to the city clerk's office to apply for a marriage license. Forty-eight hours later we walked into Central Park—my brother pushed my mother in a wheelchair, my father and Alan's family held chuppah poles, dozens of bystanders took photos with their cell phones and clenched their Starbucks coffees in their teeth as they applauded—and got married beneath an elm tree. My mother, who on leaving the hospital had gone through a brief phase of wanting desperately to have the entire wedding in her apartment (she had envisioned lush hors d'oeuvre spreads, candlelight dancing against the nighttime windowpanes, a *New York Times* wedding announcement that mentioned her art collection) and was heartbroken to finally admit it was impossible, still managed to host a gathering before the ceremony. There, at the top of the steps leading to her sunken living room, flanked by her ceramic vases and wearing jewelry from the Museum of Modern Art gift shop, she welcomed the guests and presented me with my flowers (at my insistence, tulips from the Korean grocer), the stems of which she'd wrapped in a ziplock bag to keep from dripping on my dress. This would be the last time I'd ever see her in a skirt. This would be the last time she ever set wineglasses down on a table, the last time she stood before a painting and straightened it ever so slightly against the wall. She never embarked on the kitchen renovation.

I once said, in the early days of writing these pages, "Over my dead body will this book end with a wedding." Yet here we are, with a wedding and with death, though death also seems like an unimaginative conclusion, and as I write this, my mother is still alive. There are wedding photos taped to the wall by her bed and a dizzying medication schedule and a woman from Trinidad who splits pills and opens plastic containers of applesauce and doesn't seem to fully appreciate the Franz Kline print near the piano. Back in Los Angeles, a bland, blissful city that now feels eclipsed by New York and the way our family crisis seems to ooze from every building like the smell of commercial clothes dryers emanating from basement windows, the house on Escalada Terrace lies in waiting. It waits for me to come home. It waits for us to get our act together and remove the clutter. It waits to be sold. Which it will be. We will sell the house. Maybe not immediately, but eventually. Maybe not this year, but next year. Because the house is not our house, it's my house. It may be my home but it's not really our home. Sure, Alan and I go through the motions. We live inside its walls, under its roof, over its foundation. We open and close the doors. We water the grass. We take out the trash. But do we really live here?

When I think back on the places I've lived, I now wonder this: I wonder if the real measure of "home" is the degree to which you can leave it alone. Maybe appreciating a house means knowing when to stop decorating. Maybe you've never really lived there until you've thrown its broken pieces in the garbage. Maybe learning how to be out in the big world isn't the epic journey everyone thinks it is. Maybe that's actually the easy part. The hard part is what's right in front of you. The hard part is learning how to hold the title to your very existence, to own not only property, but also your life. The hard part is learning not just how to *be* but mastering the nearly impossible art of how to be at home.

ACKNOWLEDGMENTS

For   : to
than   and
Sve   ick
Gol   ea-
tive